May God bless you sisters

Fr. Shan

I AM
in
Me

I AM
in
Me

A Mystical but Practical Application
of Eucharist in Every Stage of Life

Gnanadhas George Michael

HUDSON
HOUSE

Cover design: Brendan Davis
Interior design: Adam Wisniewski

Cataloging in Publication Data
I AM in Me
A Mystical but Practical Application of Eucharist in every Stage of Life

ISBN: 978-1-58776-919-1

1. (Religion)

Library of Congress catalog card number: 2011928817

Manufactured in the United States of America

1 2 3 4 5 6 7 8 9 10 NetPub 15 14 13 12 11

675 Dutchess Turnpike, Poughkeepsie, NY 12603
www.hudsonhousepub.com   (800) 724-1100

To my parents

George Michael, who entered into the eternal joy
of sharing the Eucharistic Banquet,

and

Maria Puspham George Michael, whose lively faith
in the Eucharist empowers me and
my two priest brothers Bellarmine and Paschal
in our commitment
to the Eucharistic Lord.

Contents

X. My Glory

Acknowledgements

I have been a priest for 33 years. For most of my priestly life in India, besides serving in parishes, I was asked to preach retreats to seminarians, nuns and lay people. The theme that ran through these retreats was always personal spirituality rooted in the Eucharistic Presence. While I was teaching Personal Spirituality in seminaries and formation houses in India, zealous students asked me to consider writing a book on personal spirituality. I would always say no because I thought that it was not in my vocation to write books. Why then, did I decide to write this book now that I am in America?

I AM In Me is born out of the influence of the parishioners of St. Mary's, Wappingers Falls, NY, where I am privileged to have served for the last seven years. It all started with their affirmation of my homilies. These affirmations are expressions of their own faith. I would categorize the affirmations that influenced this book into three significant faith expressions: First are those who affirmed, "Another inspiring homily!" This affirmation is about the Eucharistic celebration that makes sense in the light of the readings. Second are those who affirmed, "We love the way you connect the theme of every Sunday to the Eucharist." This affirmation is about their joy to rediscover the Eucharist in their daily lives. Third are those who affirmed, "Why don't you put all your homilies in writing? We would like to read them." This affirmation is about their longing to incorporate the message about the Eucharistic presence into their daily lives.

I am grateful to all the parishioners of St. Mary's, Wappingers Falls for these encouraging affirmations without them, I would not have written this book.

Ever since I thought of writing this book, the Eucharistic Lord has amazingly given me many people who helped this book a reality. I am indebted to Msgr. Francis P. Bellew, Pastor of St Mary's. His friendly and informal discussions of Sunday homilies taught me to render my Indian contextual thinking in a way acceptable and applicable to American readers. I thank him for his continuous support. The rectory staff at St Mary's: MaryAnn O'Neill and Mary Giannotti have been very helpful with their technical guidance and assistance to prepare the manuscripts; Bill Haggerty, John Fusaro, Pat Manuli, Francine Fanuele and Lucille Price have been always there with their encouraging words. I thank all of them.

I am indebted with gratitude to Dr. Ernie Valera who mentored my writing along the way. His patient reading with sensitive suggestions and corrections were an indispensable help to me in presenting the right ideas. I am grateful to Eileen Fratto and Gwen Ng for their insights that helped me to simplify theological jargons into language a lay person could grasp. Also, I am thankful to Pat LeClercq and Mary Ellen LaRose for reviewing all the chapters to correct the typo errors. I wish to express my thanks to Adam Wisniewski for editing the final phase of the book, and to Brendan Davis for designing the cover page.

I am deeply thankful to our parish community, in particular, Lou & Eilleen Fratto, Jerry & Gwen Ng, Ed & Kathi Duffy. They have been supporting me all along with their words of appreciation. I owe my gratitude to Stan & Maureen Straub, who were enthusiastic about the Eucharistic contents of the book. They introduced me to the Sacramentine Sisters in Scarsdale, NY, who are known for their perpetual adoration of the Eucharist. I owe my thanks to these nuns for their prayers and for reading through all the manuscripts to give me corrective suggestions.

My special thanks to Msgr. William J. Belford for the Preface to this book. I consider his insights more valuable than the book.

I express my gratitude to all those I interviewed regarding each topic. Your stories are inspirational starters for each topic. May your life and witness be the source of inspiration to all the readers.

Lastly, but not the least, I am joyfully grateful to the mystical presence of I AM in the Eucharist for all these blessings. May these meditations bring all praise and glory to the Eucharistic presence that forms us into the great mystery of the Body of Christ.

Preface

I have enjoyed this interesting and inspiring collection of 52 meditations on the relationship of Christ and the Eucharist to us, his holy people, as we journey from our origins to our eternal life.

A priest of some 33 years, with experience of India and America, Fr. Dhas illumines and shares his cultures in the universal pursuit of personal spirituality that leads to greater peace and joy.

The opening part of each chapter tells us a story of beautiful encounters and experiences that lead into Fr. Dhas' Eucharistic insights. He draws upon Scripture and brings forth words of God that we overlook or forget. He helps us to realize more deeply our gift of Holy Communion and of the Eucharistic presence of Our Lord.

I found that Father weaves the words and questions of his parishioners into tapestry of easily understood lessons about the awesome mystery of God with us, of Jesus as the Bread of our lives. In our secular environment, there is great importance for people to know and clergy to preach the tremendous effect of welcoming Jesus, of having Jesus with us in the Eucharist.

Some books and homilies try to be so brilliant that they discourage people and cannot be understood. Father Dhas draws us in with familiar examples and recognizable issues. Then he gives understandable, comforting advice for our worries and concerns.

An example concerns sin and forgiveness. An admiral's question reflects the worry many people have that they will be denied heaven. Father makes the Pauline point that we don't know why we sin. But God does know everything-and with understanding comes forgiveness.

I can see why his fellow priests and parishioners hold Fr. Dhas in such high esteem. And I heartily encourage lay people and clergy to get this book for their own meditation. Then they can keep it nearby and use it for sharing hope and joy on our Eucharistic journey to the banquet of heaven.

Msgr. William J. Belford,
Vicar for Clergy, NY Archdiocese

Introduction

This book is meant for anyone who would like to revisit each event of his/her life in the light of the Eucharistic presence. There are 52 chapters (one for each week) in the book, which highlight the course of every event from birth to eternal life. In order to present a realistic approach to every event of our life, each chapter begins with a short description of a concrete life experience, or a related interview of a person, or of some facts. So each first section is intended as a starting point to invite the reader to associate life's events with the true stories of others.

The second section will proceed to establish the biblical context of the chapter. I tried to avoid theological jargon so as to present it in a simple way for the reader. The biblical basis will provide the reader the needed relevance of God's Word to each event in order to establish the connection between every human event and Christ. The reader has to identify his/her life event with every stage of growth and fulfillment of the incarnate Son of God. The caption of each chapter is such that it will help identify one's life event with that of Jesus. The reader is invited to re-align his/her past events with those of Jesus.

The third section will guide the reader to his or her own personal context of life in the biblical context of the Eucharistic Presence. It is here that the reader has to delve into mystical and ecclesial dimensions of the Eucharist. It will establish that one's life is inherently mystical because of the Eucharistic presence. Mysticism is not just an esoteric experience as we used to think in the past; it is an experience of anyone who is aware of God's presence in them.

The last section will suggest the reader to engage in meditation. It advocates the technique of *Breathing*; conscious breathing makes us aware of our inner self that has already become the tabernacle for Christ. It will also outline two techniques of meditation, one in the church and the other in the home; this will be the end of each chapter. Meditation is not necessarily to be experienced as a heightened consciousness of one's self; it is a simple but natural way of experiencing the Eucharistic Lord within. At the end of the mediation, the reader is given a verse from the Psalms, intended for musing throughout the entire week.

In all these sections what is interwoven is a personal spirituality. It takes into account the random sayings: "Many are "religious," but not 'spiritual." Or "Some are "spiritual" but not "religious." One is characterized as "Religious," when he or she goes to church, receives the sacraments, observes certain norms of the church, and attends Mass to fulfill the Eucharistic obligation. On the other hand, one is "spiritual," when he or she leads a good life, but cares less about being "religious."

"Religious" without being "spiritual" makes one just a performer, usually ending in hypocrisy. "Spiritual" without being "religious" will become self-conceit, that is harmful to oneself and to others in the long run. So I believe personal spirituality is the key. This book encourages one to grow in personal spirituality that integrates both the spiritual and religious realm of spirituality. Personal spirituality can never be selfish in action. As it is mystical, its effect is a witness for the church and for the society.

This book will awake the reader to the wake up call of Pope Benedict. XVI, *How great is humanity's need today to rediscover the source of its hope in the Sacrament of the Eucharist*. Many scholars have undertaken the task of rediscovering the power of the Eucharist. They are God's numerous stars. It is my sincere hope this book will place, as Indian Poet Tagore would say, "my little lamp amidst the numerous stars."

Suggestion for Meditation

In the Church:

- Be seated in a comfortable pew, begin to focus your eyes on the Tabernacle for a while.

- Be conscious of your presence in front of Jesus in the Tabernacle, close your eyes, be conscious of your breath for a minute or two, until you get the feeling of a self-awareness. *(Consciousness of your breath will create in you an awareness of inner self of your body.)*

- Be conscious of your inner self that has become the Tabernacle.

- Invite Jesus into the inner self by consciously breathing in and let the natural flow of inhaling and exhaling continue for few seconds.

- Bring to your mind what you have read from the Personal Context of the Chapter; make it very personal. This may continue for about five minutes.

- Take a deep breath in and out just to relax your body. Bend your head towards your chest to say few words of thanks to Jesus who is within you.

In the Home:

- Choose a comfortable place to be seated, be conscious of a visual picture of the church you go to and the place of the tabernacle. The Lord's presence in the tabernacle reaches the ends of the earth, so also it reaches your home and you.

- Close your eyes, be conscious of your breath for a minute or two, until your get the feeling of self-awareness.

- Be conscious of your inner self that has become the Tabernacle.

Follow the same steps suggested above

I. My Origin

1. I Am Part of the Horizon of 'Before'

You are not an accident that just happened.
You were planned by the Father and
conceived through the miracle of Divine
love.
Patricia A. McLaughlin[1]

One First Holy Communion celebration of the second graders of St. Mary's School, Wappingers Falls, took place on May 19, 2009.It was a memorable one. All the children were remarkable in their participation at the Mass. Among them was one Kaitlyn, who was in the very first pew from the altar. Kaitlyn's way of responding to the prayers and singing the songs stood out so much. Just before the communion service, the First Communicants were singing the popular song: **Come to Me, Come to Me, Jesus said Come to Me.** *At that moment, I watched Kaitlyn's parents; Michael and Theresa become very emotional with tears of joy to be one with their daughter's singing. This led me to find out more about Kaitlyn and her parents.*

They have been married for 14 years, and they revere their marriage as a beautiful sacrament that makes them so responsible to each other and to their child. Their focus is on the child all the time. They said they pray every evening. The three take turns praying for themselves and for various intentions of the day. They added that Sunday Eucharist for them is the way of living their faith and commitment to each other. Every year on

1

their wedding anniversary they make it a point to view their wedding video and thank God for the sacrament that united them. Now that Kaitlyn joins them to enjoy the video, it becomes all the more a reality to witness to the Sacrament of God's love.

Michael and Theresa say, "Kaitlyn is our blessing." One time at the age of three, Kaitlyn told her parents, "It was God who sent me to you. God gave me a big hug before sending me to you." It looks like the parents recall this message all the time when they say, "Kaitlyn is a gift to us from God." Michael says, "It is the purity of the child and the truth she reveals is amazing to us." Michael and Theresa are one of thousands and thousands of parents who have the glimpse of the horizon of "before." They take the birth and life of their children so seriously so as to continue God's purpose in their lives.

We know from the life experience of all the biblical personalities that there is a larger mystery that surrounds our birth and life. For example, Isaiah marveled at this mystery, "The Lord called me from birth, from my mother's womb" (Is 49:1). Jeremiah records God's words of this mystery, "Before I formed you in the womb I knew you, before you were born I dedicated you" (Jer 1:5). "Calling" from birth, "forming" in the womb, and "knowing" before the birth tell us about the eternity of our origin. Jeremiah, Isaiah, and others in the biblical history comprehended that they were part of this mystery. That is why they valued their birth as something eternal so as to fit into the plan of God for them.

The idea of eternity is a mystery because of its horizon of "before" and "after" life. The horizon is never comprehensible to the human mind, and so it remains a mystery. Mystery in Christian understanding is not something unreal; it is real to the human mind. It is real because it enables one to see the plan of God in all the life events of our birth, upbringing, education, work, vocation, witness, worship, death, and resurrection. These events lie between the horizon of "before" and "after." All human beings are called to participate in all these events according to the plan of God. It is in this participation we realize that we are a part of the mystery of the "before" and "after."

St. John, the beloved disciple, was particularly adept at grasping eternity to our origin. He began his gospel with the phrase, "In the beginning." Probably, fascinated by the first words of the book of Genesis, he proceeded to write, "In the beginning was the Word, and the Word was with God, and the Word was God" (Jn 1:1). Again, he reiterated the phrase in verse 2, "He was in the beginning with God," in order to reveal the fact all things came to be through Jesus Christ, who was there before the world came to be. St. Paul will take up the horizon of "before," brought out by St. John.

St. Paul's acclamation of eternity very convincingly tells us that we were chosen in Christ before the foundation of the world. "Blessed be the God and Father of Our Lord Jesus Christ who has blessed us in Christ with every spiritual blessing in the heavens as he chose us in him before the foundation of the world" (Eph 1:3, 4). We were chosen in Him before the world came to be, which means our birth had a beginning in eternity. Simply put, we were "conceived" in the mind of God before we were conceived in the womb of our mother. Again, Jesus' own birth, life, and mission attributed eternal value to our own birth. It is in Him we know that God has a plan for each of us even before the world was created. Accordingly, our birth did not happen accidentally; it is to fulfil the eternal plan of God.

St. Paul comprehended the mystery of our birth and argued if we are chosen in Him, we also live in Him and for Him (cf. Col 1:16, 1Cor 8:6). It is one thing to know that we are chosen in Him, who was there from all eternity. It is another thing to participate in his plan. We should choose to live with Him here on earth and in the next. Jesus says "Just as the living Father sends me and I have life because of the Father, so also the one who feeds on me will have life" (Jn 6:57). Feeding on the Eucharist is what makes us participate in the life of Jesus now, in order to be with Jesus forever; it is like an eternal thread that binds our birth, our life, and our life eternal. That is why Jesus said, "Whoever eats my flesh and drinks my blood has eternal life" (Jn 6:54).

My Personal Context:

How shall I acknowledge the plan of God for me? Let me go into myself. I am not here in this world accidentally. God knew me. God chose me. He created me to be His in the world in order to be with him forever. Jesus dwells in me ever since I received the Eucharist. Now that Jesus dwells within me, let me remind myself of my chosen birth; let me honor my life as blessed; let me assure myself of His assurance: "Come, you who are blessed by my Father, inherit the Kingdom prepared for you from the foundation of the world" (Mt 25:34). So, the life I have is not about me, but about Jesus in me. Let me decide to participate consciously in His life and to live for him all the time.

Meditation:

After the preparatory steps:

I am conscious of my Breathing. I am conscious of Jesus' presence in me; let me become intimate with my breathing now; Jesus' presence in me enables me to know that I have participated in God's mystery. This did not happen by chance; I was known and chosen even before I was born. And so, let me pray: *This is amazing Lord, to know that You had chosen me. Help me never to take my life for granted. Let me join the Psalmist to sing the whole day:*

You formed my inmost being;
You knit me in my mother's womb.
I praise you, so wonderfully you made me;
Wonderful are your works (139:13).

2. I Am the Image of God

My life is not about me. It is about my
willing participation in large mystery.

Richard Rohr[1]

One year I joined the silent protest of the Respect Life group of our parish to stand with inspiring posters depicting the evil of abortion for the commuters to read. We received supporting gestures. There were a few negative comments; one of them was from a young lady seated with another young lady driving; she shouted: "you don't have to tell me what I have to do with my life; go home!" I was almost impelled to shout back to her, but we were asked to accept any sort of reaction; instead we were asked to be gracious. Yet I said within me: "Lady, life is not about you; it is about you and God; you cannot say that you can do anything with your life."

Every life begins and ends with God. Between the beginning and the end of our life, the life is meant to be with God, for God. It is all because we are the image of God. Everyone comes into the world to be the image of God. When the author of Genesis writes about the creation, he recognizes the special creation of man in the Image of God:

God created man in his image;

In the divine image he created him;

7

Male and female he created them (Gen 1:27).
Interpretation of this text should recognize the fact every man, every women is created in the divine image.

What is Image? The Hebrew word for Image is *tselem;* that means shape, shadow, resemblance, figure, not abstract, but real; in as much as man is real, he is image of God. The common understanding of image is attributed to figure or shape. But God has no shape or figure; God is spirit. If so, what is God's image in man? It is the SOUL, that makes him the image of God. The catechism of the Catholic Church describes it so well: "The term Soul often refers to human life or the entire human person. But "soul" also refers to the innermost aspect of man that which is of greatest value in him, that by which he is most especially in God's Image: "soul" signifies the spiritual principle in man" (363). While theologians say "Soul", Psychology refers to it as the "self."

The Hebrew word *Naphesh* and the Greek word *Psyche* for the soul was widely used to mean life, living creature, emotions etc (Gen 2:7, Ps 6:4), but when it is used for a person, it refers to the animating principle of life: the soul or self. Also, it might be of interest to know that the Greek word for life, *bios*, is frequently used as equivalent word for *Psyche*. That means whether we call life, the soul or the self it is one and the same in Greek understanding. Various branches of Philosophy describe self as Interiority, Inner-self, Inner-domain, Inner-awareness, Self-consciousness, Inner-person, etc. All these refer to the Soul or the Self, which is the Image of God. In the context of this chapter we shall prefer the word "Self" to "Soul."

God creating man endows him with SELF. And so man becomes self-conscious. Self-consciousness makes a person to know he is not just a bundle of emotion. He is more than that. Self makes him first of all aware of the reality that he is distinct from other things and persons. Secondly it awakens him to the "self- realization" of who he is; He realizes that He is what he is because of God's Presence within him. Man alone has the self realization to say, "Oh God you are within me." No other creatures on earth can say that. With this self realization begins the process of the image of God. Image of God is the life within. Life is not passive nor is it inactive. It is dynamic in its interaction. God's life-*as the Image of God*- makes one interact with God within and with others.

Self-realization of Jesus is evidenced in the compelling sayings of Jesus himself: "The Father is in me and I am in the Father" (Jn 10:38, 14:11). The self-realization of Jesus makes Jesus acknowledge the process of the Father "working" in him. That is why Jesus says, "The Father who dwells in me is doing his works. Believe me that I am in the Father and the Father is in me, or else, believe because of the works themselves" (Jn

14:10b,11). This is evidently the process which the Image of God does   in all of us.

When we "self-realize" that God is within us, the image of God within us begin to interact, with God first, and then with others. Our self-realization is about Jesus within us. And the interaction between Jesus and us is always working. Most importantly, our own self is more evident in its realization because of the Eucharistic presence of Jesus within us. Jesus says, "Just as the living Father sent me and I have life because of the Father, so also the one who feeds on me will have life because of me" (Jn 6:57). It is no wonder why Jesus proclaimed himself as "the bread of Life" (Jn 6:48). Jesus as the Bread of life offers us life.

In the context of Jesus coming to abide within us, the mystics and the saints describe the beauty of the soul. St. Catherine of Siena exclaims, "What tastes and sees and touches this sacrament? The soul's sensitivity."[2] St. Julian of Norwich understands soul as the "Glorious City! In the midst of that city sits Our Lord Jesus, God and man."[3] St Bede calls the soul as "A great inner sanctum, a sweet sacred place!"[4] Thus we see the very interactive presence of Jesus in the Eucharist animating every human person who "realizes" His abiding Presence.

It is in receiving the Eucharist, Jesus, the perfect image of God that make us sharers of God's own life in us. As Pope

Benedict puts it, "It is in Jesus... we have become sharers of God's inmost life. Jesus Christ... makes us in the gift of the Eucharist, sharers in Gods own life."[5] And so, whenever we receive Jesus, we are conscious of our own self-awakening to His Presence in us.

My Personal Context:

I am the image of God because of my Self, the soul, the life of God in me. It is within me that I can experience my God, whose Image I am destined to be from the creation; I am awakened to the Image of God when I receive Jesus in the Eucharist. It is so fulfilling to receive the Eucharist, and I am conscious of my self, relating to Jesus, the perfect image of God in me. And so, it is no more my self, but God's Self in and through Christ in me. I am willing now to participate in this great life.

Meditation:

After the preparatory steps:

I am conscious of my own Self as the image of God; I am conscious of Jesus, the perfect image of God making me all the more into His image. I rejoice within myself to pray: *Jesus, my Soul, my Self, and my Life I thank you for creating me in your own image. You are my soul. You are my self. You are my life. Let me rejoice with your Eucharistic presence to sing along with the Psalmist the whole day*

Bless the lord, my soul;

All my being, bless his holy name.

Bless the lord, my soul

Do not forget all the gifts of God (103:1,2).

3. I Am Born to Relate to God

Jesus' image of God was decidedly personal. God was his *Abba* Father.... His God was an infinitely loving and intimate person.

Albert Nolan[1]

Gene is a young dad with three children, Gianna, Eugene and Vincenzo. His wife Mia diagnosed with M.S. (Multiple Sclerosis) is being treated with multiple treatments. In spite of his care and duty to be around Mia, Gene is there every Sunday in the church without fail. He brings Gianna and Eugene with him to church. Knowing his love and concern for Mia, especially what he is going through with a series of tests and treatments, everyone asks, "How is Mia? Before he replies, I watch his tears to say, "Fine for now." As he finds it difficult to answer to the obvious questions that everyone asks him about Mia, he wrote to us priests, to explain all about Mia's medical tests and treatment.

I was moved to read, "With our little ones, Gianna, Eugene and Vincenzo at home, our lives and future suddenly in havoc and our minds spinning out of control, I ask God's help to keep me strong for everybody." It is moving to hear about his realistic admiration for Mia. In spite of the deadly brain infection, and the noticeable symptoms of extreme tiredness, Gene writes, "What she does for the children I can never do. She's amazing!" About his trust in God, he writes, "I've always believed in God's will and taking whatever comes my way in stride; that mentality always served me well, but it is hard to apply it to my loved ones and what we are going through now."

Gene's love for his wife and little children leaves within me lots of reflective musings: *Where does this sort of selfless care come from? Is it just an instinct? What is the origin of goodness in every person?* These and other reflections take us to the basic understanding of who a person is.

According to Abraham J. Heschel, one of the famous OT scholars, a person's presence is what makes one a person. He says, "Of a person whose out-wardness communicates something of his indwelling power or greatness, whose soul is radiant and conveys itself without words, we say he has presence."[2] In other words, one is admired as a "person" when others experience his or her goodness. Thus a *person* is the one who has the goodness to share his own goods with others.

What is in the understanding of God as a person? Inasmuch as the goodness is a gift from God, it also helps us understand who God is. God is a person. Celebrating God as a person should not treat God as one among many persons. We celebrate God as person because he is personal. Albert Nolan, a renowned spiritual author suggests, "Perhaps it is better to say that the mystery we call God is personal rather than *a* person."[3] God is personal as we relate to Him for the goodness of His Presence.

God's goodness is visible in the world. In the old Anglo-Saxon English, the word God means good; God is good. The linguistic explanation of El and Elohim for God is so amazing; it expresses the personal character of God to relate to others. God is conscious of His Self to share His goodness with creation; it is evidently manifested in the very first act of God as creator. At the end of every act of creation, God saw how good it was. This delight of God is an approval on the part of God to have shared His goodness with the creation.

His goodness is manifested in man as he is created with the power of self. The creation of man powerfully manifests the goodness of God. "Self" in man makes him relate to God as a person. That is the reason the psalmist praises God "He fills the earth with goodness" (Ps 33:5). "Give thanks to the Lord, who is good, whose love endures for ever" (Ps 118:1). Even to implore God's mercy, man relates to His goodness: "The Lord is good to all, compassionate to every creature" (Ps 145:9). "Have mercy on me God in your goodness" (Ps 51:1).

The greatest act by which God manifested Himself a Person was by sharing His goodness in sending His own son: " God sent his only Son into the world so that we might have life through him"(1Jn 4:10b). Jesus, realizing within himself the personal love of the Father loved us. "As the Father loves me, so I also love you" (Jn 15 9). The goodness of the Father led Jesus to embrace the sacrifice of his life on the cross. The Goodness of the Father raised him to life. St. John, the beloved disciple of Jesus, earnestly proclaims that our goodness rests on God's goodness: "We love because He first loved us" (Jn 4:19). This remarkable statement makes it so evident how God relates with us as a personal God, and that we have become personal in our relationship with God and neighbors. So, it is the presence of His goodness that makes God so personal to us. We relate to God's Presence in the Eucharist.

The Eucharistic Presence of Jesus is the summit of Gods goodness for us. Jesus at the institution of the Eucharist testifies to the personal goodness of His Father: "Just as the living Father sent me and I have life because of the Father, so also the one who feeds on me will have life because of me"(Jn 6:57). St. Ignatius of Antioch, one of the first early Christian witnesses to the Eucharist makes a captivating memoir: "The Eucharist is the selfsame body, which was nailed to the cross, which suffered for our sins and which the Father with His goodness raised up" (Epistle to the Smyrnaeans 7). So in the Eucharistic Presence of Jesus our soul can relate to the very person of Jesus, the perfect image of God.

My Personal Context:

I am the image of God.... I am created a person because of God's own goodness to relate with me.... What makes me a person is my Self, which is the Image of God.....I am awakened to

God's Presence within me…. It relates to me in a personal way as if I am the only person on earth…. It is an awesome feeling to relate to Jesus. St. John's experience *"to have heard, to have seen, to have touched"* Jesus is mine now. And so, I too "may have fellowship with the Father, and with His son, Jesus Christ" (1Jn 1:3). I have this fellowship with Jesus in the Eucharist…. I see. I hear… I touch… I join St. Julian of Norwich in praising the Lord, "the exalted goodness of the Trinity is our Lord and in Him we are enclosed and He in us" (Ch 54, *The Joy of God in us*).

Meditation:

After the preparatory steps:

Jesus is the person in me; Jesus and I are one. I rejoice within me to pray: *Jesus, my Lord, and my Image I thank you for creating me in your own Image. From the time I received your Body within me, I know that you are in me as my own self. Let me thank you for this fellowship. Let me join the Psalmist to sing the whole day:*

How good our God has been to me! (13:6d).

4. I Am Transformed into His Likeness

God supports and honors his image within
us because it reflects his own goodness.
Thomas Keating[1]

It was in one of the Homes for the aged run by the Sisters of the Poor; I met with the strange reaction of an elderly man, who was Hindu. He was 80 years old then; during his life he admits, he was rowdy, arrogant, bossy, and disrespectful to his wife and to all in the family. The consequence was that he was totally disowned by all in the family and at the end they threw him out into street, Thanks to the good sisters he ended up in the Home for the aged. This is where I ran into him; he stopped me to say, "Father, I feel so ashamed of myself. I am treated so well here; I don't deserve it at all. The sisters are so good, smiling caring." I mentioned, "You are in the right place." With the shame in his face and tears in his eyes he said, "I was all through my life a terror to others; here I see the Sisters so humble, caring for me, and the more I am cared for, the more I feel guilty about my life."

His guilt was such that one day he asked a sister, "Why are you so good to me?" The response was in action to point out to him the Lord in the Eucharist. The story of this man ended with his receiving Baptism and the Eucharist before he entered into eternal rest. Here is an example of a man whose image once was never transformed into the likeness; the kindness of the Sisters of the Poor brought him to the senses of his own image. He was ashamed of his past, but was transformed by the very act of goodness of the sisters.

The good news: "Let us make man in our image, after our likeness" from the book of Genesis (1:26) has been the subject of study for many scholars; so much has been written about *Image and likeness*. It is the most fundamental truth to understand the dignity of man. We have to learn more and more about our image and to establish the dignity of ours and those of others.

Though **image and likeness** are used identically to mean one and the same concept, they are clearly two distinct Hebrew words: *tselem* for image and *demuth* for likeness. There seems to be an inconsistent usage of these words when the author of Genesis uses only the word Image in 1:27 "God created man in His *image*," and uses only the word *likeness* in 5:1 "When God created man, he made him in the *likeness* of God." Moreover the words are used in different order to write about Adam's son in 5:3 "When he begot a son *in his likeness* and, *after his image*." These and other identical and interchangeable use of the words of Old Testament context can be better understood in the light of the New Testament context.

Jesus' incarnation was God's recognition of the image of man. At the incarnation, as St. John puts it, "No one has ever seen God. The only Son, God, who is at the Father's side, has revealed him" (Jn 1:18). Man looking at the image of the Son of God came to the realization of his own image and dignity. The dignity depends on the transformation of his image into the likeness of God. It is one thing to have the image of God; it is another thing to become the likeness of God. Inasmuch as we see the image of God in us, we also see it's transformational nature. Our image is transformed into His likeness.

St. Paul envisions this transformation as tied to Jesus Himself. Our image, according to St. Paul, is "conformed to the image of His son" (Rom 8:29a). It is because we "are being transformed into the same image" (2Cor 3:18), and so we "have to put on a new self, which is being renewed, for knowledge in the image of its creator" (Col 3:10). "Being transformed" or "Being renewed" entails a process of becoming "His likeness." Inasmuch as there is awareness in every human being to participate in the process, one cannot comprehend the ways of this process; yet it is real. That is why we call this process as mystical process. Mystical process begins with an awareness of the indwelling presence of God in us. It becomes a doorway to the process of transformation.

St. John brings in the idea of the mystical process when he says that God's love is "truly perfected in us" (1Jn 2:5). Love here is not a concept for our mind. Rather it is an experience of

God's presence in us. "God remains in us, and his love is brought to perfection in us" (1Jn 4:12). His presence in us respects and supports His image in us. The support God offers us is what becomes the power to make His image into His likeness. So the "Image" itself is up to the process of renewal, that is, becoming God's "likeness."

In order to grasp the mystical transformation of *Image* into *Likeness* we need to understand the power of Mind. Endowed with the power of Mind- *knowledge, reason, responsibility, freedom*- we are able to have an awareness of God indwelling in us. With *knowledge*, we are aware of the indwelling presence of God in us. With *reason*, we are able to convince ourselves of that indwelling presence of God in us. With *responsibility*, we consent to participate in the process of becoming the likeness of God. And, with *freedom*, we choose between the process of becoming the likeness of God and enslaving to the ego. If we choose to use less of all these faculties, we become useless. In other words, we choose to prefer the ego that enslaves us to the Presence of God that supports and honors us. The ego in us does not care about the Image one way or other.

The word 'transformation' is the translation of the Greek word 'Morphe' which stands for inward change. Inner change does not happen magically, but starts with the self-awareness of who we are. It is a process. As Willigis Jager, Benedictine monk and one of the spiritual leaders would say, "We are here to become true human beings, by going beyond our individual egos, and to realize that our true essence is the essence of God.... Give yourself over to this process of life and trust that it is God's process."[2] Our awareness instills in us this process of my own self-becoming God- self. It is this awareness that tells me that God- self embraces my ego within me; and so, I don't act under the dictate of my ego. My ego itself becomes aware of my God - self to do and say everything, as Christ would do.

Everyone enters into the process with an awareness of the presence of Jesus in us. One should be aware of the coming of Jesus into us in the Eucharist. Pope Benedict XVI describes this process: "The Eucharist, since it embraces the concrete, everyday existence of the believer, makes possible, day by day, the progressive transfiguration of all those called by grace to reflect the image of the son of God."[3] 'Transfiguration' is a biblical word to denote the transformational process.

My Personal Context:

Let me be aware of the image of God in me; the "image" has to be transfigured into His likeness. The likeness is nothing but Christ-likeness. It is by the reception of the Eucharist I am being transfigured into the likeness of Christ. With the power of mind, let me decide to cooperate with the presence of Jesus to go through the process. Let me begin the process by the frequent reception of the Eucharist.

Meditation:

After the preparatory steps:

I have breathed my Jesus into me. Let this awareness increase in me my likeness to Christ. I am so thankful to Jesus for the transformation that is taking place within me. Let me join the Psalmist to sing within me the whole day.

When I awake, let me be filled with your presence (Ps 17:15).

5. I Am God's Glory

The glory of God is the living man.
And the life of man is the vision of God.
St Irenaeus[1]

Msgr. Frank Bellew, Pastor of St.Marys Church told me of his installation as pastor of St. Mary's Church, Wappingers Falls, NY. At the end of the Installation mass, the choir sang the famous song, "How great thou art." The installed pastor said to the presiding Bishop, "I love this song." But the Bishop made a joke out of it to tell the new pastor, "Remember, Frank, 'How great thou art'- is not about you, but about God." The priests who listened to the fun enjoyed the sense of humor. When it was told to me, it occurred to me to say, "Wait a minute! The greatness of God is shining through the greatness of man and the greatness of man is the glory of God."

The word, 'glory' is the translation of the Hebrew word 'Shechinah', which comes from the root Shechan, which means 'to dwell'. God's glory 'dwells' in the heavens: "The Heavens declare the Glory of God" (Ps 19:2a). God's glory 'dwells' in the earth: "All the earth is filled with His glory" (Is 6:3). God's glory 'dwells' in the temple: "the glory of God filled the Dwelling" (Ex 40:34). God's glory 'dwells' in humans: "You have made them little less than a god, crowned them with glory and honor" (Ps 8:6). Abraham Heschel, one of the most revered scholars of

25

Jewish theology, discusses that the Glory of God really means the Presence of God. He says, "It means the whole earth is full of His presence." According to him, "The whole earth is full of His glory, but we do not perceive it; it is within our reach, but beyond our grasp."[2] Inasmuch as God's presence fills the earth, we cannot perceive it, but we know for sure it is within our reach to experience it.

The glory of God is *within our reach* when we see the beauty of creation. It is *within our reach* when we go to the temple. These experiences are outside of us. Only when the glory of God becomes our own experience we can truly say it is *within our reach*. God's Presence was there in the humans from the beginning, but it was invisible to the humans. As St. John testifies, "What was from the beginning, what we have heard, what we have seen with our eyes, what we looked upon and touched with our hands concerns the Word of life... was made visible to us" (1Jn 1:1, 2).The Incarnation of Jesus made it possible for us to see the glory of God as Jesus is visible Glory of God.

Contemplating on the incarnation of God, St. Paul tells us that the incarnation was God's own plan to make us, humans, to become God's glory. He says, "In him we are chosen, destined in accord with the purpose of the one who accomplishes all things according to the intention of His will, so that we might exist for the praise of His Glory"(Eph 1:11,12). He says in his letter to the Colossians, "to whom God chose to make known the riches of the glory of this mystery among the Gentiles; it is Christ in you, the hope for glory" (Col 1:27). It is in the Eucharist that we experience the glory of Christ's presence. When we receive Jesus, we have his glory within us. Now we can say Jesus is within our reach.

My scripture professor, Fr. Lucien Legrand, one of the international scholars of Johannine Theology, is the man who formed and informed many of us to take the profound reality of the Eucharist to the very heart of our priestly life. He preferred the word 'tabernacle' to 'dwelling'. He argued that the mystery of Incarnation itself is an obvious reference to the Eucharist; for instance of Jn 1:14, he would use the word, "tabernacle."

"And the Word became flesh

and *tabernacled* among us,

and we saw his glory"

The amazing prayer of Jesus to His Father: "I have given them the Glory that you gave me so that they may be one as we are one, I in them and you in me..." (Jn 17: 22, 23). The oneness is brought about by Jesus' indwelling in all us in the Eucharist. He has tabernacled in us, and thus Jesus is glorified in us: "Everything of mine is yours and everything of yours is mine, and I have been glorified in them" (Jn 17:10). We have become partakers of his glory by His abiding Presence in us.

St. Iraneus grasped the Glory of God as giving life; the life assured by Jesus: "I am the Bread of Life; whoever comes to me will never hunger, and whoever believes in me will never thirst" (Jn 6:35). Jesus' assurance is an invitation for us to come to him and to believe in him. In other words those who see the life in the Bread and receive the Bread will have life. That is why St Iraneus says, "The Glory of God gives life; those who see God receive life. For this reason God, who cannot be grasped, comprehended, or seen, allows himself to be seen, comprehended and grasped by men, that may He give life to those who see and receive him."[3] We can certainly conclude the purpose of the creation of humans was to make them the abode of God's Presence. We share His glory by receiving the Eucharist into us.

My Personal Context:

I can certainly conclude that the purpose of my life here on earth is to participate in Gods glory; the glory itself is an attribute of His presence in me. This enhances the beauty of my participation at the Eucharistic liturgy. What Pope Benedict XVI says to me is remarkable: "The beauty of the liturgy is part of this mystery; it is a sublime expression of God's glory and, in a certain sense, a glimpse of heaven on earth."[4]

Meditation:

After the preparatory steps:

I am conscious of the glory that has been bestowed on me even before I was born; This is God's vision for my life that I should manifest His glory.; I shall continue to be conscious of His presence as I begin to pray: *Jesus I am conscious of your presence in me; because of your presence in me, I have God s glory in me; Let me manifest your glory in all I say and do. I shall join the Psalmist to sing of the ways of the Lord:*

How great is the Glory of the Lord! (138:5).

6. I Am Unique for God

The idea that God has created each
individual human being is essential to the
Bible's image of man. Every human being
is unique, and willed as such by God.

Pope Benedict, XVI[1]

A few years ago, I was invited to preach retreat to a group of diocesan clergy. On the very first day, before we began the retreat, one of the priests introduced himself to tell me, "Father, This may be my last retreat as a priest; I am here to decide whether or not I should continue to be a priest." He briefed me about some of his difficulties. His predicament was all the time before me, and so I vowed within myself to win him to his vocation. And so, I did devote a conference to the Uniqueness of each priest, to prove the fact that no priest is a carbon copy of the other to God; no other priest can fill in for what he can do, and so each of us is needed for God. To make a long story short, at the end of the retreat he came to tell me that he decided to stay a priest. And he is still a happy priest.

In ordinary parlance, when we speak of the uniqueness of each man and woman, we refer to physical, emotional and behavioral traits that are special to each one. But in the biblical context it refers to a person's interior disposition that affiliates with God. What the Lord said to Samuel: "Not as man sees does God see, because man sees the appearance but the Lord looks

31

into the heart" (1Sam 16:7) is particularly inspiring to understand the interiority of every person.

Interiority is the internal awareness that has the potential to open one up to the special plan of God. The Lord said to Jeremiah, "For I know well the plans I have in mind for you, plans for your welfare, plans to give a future full of hope"(Jer 29:11). In the Wisdom book, Job offers a lucid understanding of why he would open up his interiority to God's plan: "I know that you can do all things, and that no purpose of yours can be hindered. I have dealt with great things that I do not understand; things too wonderful for me, which I cannot know" (Jb 42:2,3). These words of Job help us understand his unique manner of trusting God. The popular saying, "God made you the way you are for a reason" says it all. That is, each of us has different ways of opening up our interiority to discern God's plan.

Even though the OT refers to the whole nation as chosen by God, yet people's mindset was that each and every person was uniquely chosen. Even referring to their fathers, for example, Azariah would say, "For the sake of Abraham, *your beloved*, Isaac, *your servant*, Israel, *your holy one...*" (Dan 3:35). Abraham knew that he had to be God's *beloved* more than anything else. Isaac knew he should be God's *servant* more than anything else. Israel knew that he had to be the *holy one* more than anything else. So too, God's plan for each of us is different from that of others, and that is what makes each of us unique.

Jesus himself was testifying to his own uniqueness in this marvelous passage: "The Father who dwells in me is doing his works" (Jn 14:11). His words, 'dwells in me' refer to his interiority, and 'doing his works' refer to his mission. These are distinctive sayings of Jesus testifying to the fact that the uniqueness comes from God. The interiority of Jesus is not only affiliated with God, but also draws its uniqueness from His Father to do His Father's work. Each of us draws our uniqueness from God.

Jesus was perfectly aware of the uniqueness of each one of his Apostles. In other words, Jesus was aware of the depth of their interiority. For example, Jesus renamed Simon as Peter as he knew He alone could be the Rock. Each of them was different. Yet each of them was needed for Jesus because of their own uniqueness. Jesus' approach to their uniqueness was evident in the way he instructed them: "You know that the rulers of the Gentiles lord it over them, and the great ones make their authority over them felt. But it shall not be among you" (Mt 20:25,26a). Jesus never wanted them to compare themselves nor to compete with each other. The Apostles realized that each one had his own uniqueness to do the mission of their Lord. This is what made Peter, James and John the unique "three" to be with Jesus at the important moments. And this is what made John to think of himself "the beloved" Apostle.

St. Paul bolsters up his call as unique when compared to that of other apostles: "For I am in no way inferior to these "superapostles," even though I am nothing" (2 Cor 12:11). He recognizes his uniqueness coming from God through Jesus, "God, who from my mothers womb had set me apart and called me through his grace, was pleased to reveal his Son to me"(Gal 1:15). He would acknowledge his uniqueness of his call to be an "Apostle."

St Paul explains the uniqueness of each of us in the metaphor of a human body: "For as in one body we have many parts, and all the parts do not have the same functions, so we, though many, are one body in Christ and individually parts of one another" (Rom 12:4,5). He encourages all of us to be a unique part of Christ's body as a head, as a hand, as an eye, as feet, as God intended (cf. 1 Cor Chapter12). None of us should be reduced to a mere 'one among many' in the world. Each of us is known and called personally to be a unique part of His body.

It is in receiving the Eucharist each of us revitalizes our own interiority to be open to God, to His relationship. Jesus expressed it as an analogy: He is the vine and each of us is a branch; though all the branches look apparently same, each is unique and the uniqueness comes from the Lord: "I am the vine, you are the branches. Whoever remains in me and I in him will bear much fruit, because without me you can do nothing" (Jn 15:5). So, the interiority of each one derives its strength from the Eucharist, and the strength of the uniqueness depends on the measure by which we are connected with the Lord in the Eucharist.

My Personal Context:

I am a unique person. As Albert Nolan puts it, "There has never been, and there never will be an individual person like me- or like you."[2] As I am aware of my own interiority so do I realize that it has to open itself constantly to the Lord. I am like any OT prophet or St Paul or any other person, chosen by God to do what others cannot do. What I alone can do for God is the plan of God for me. Let me accept it and live my call.

Meditation:

After the preparatory steps:

When I am conscious of my interiority, I am aware of its need to be open to Jesus. He is in me to do my work as the Father was in Jesus to do His work. Let me pray: *Jesus I am conscious of your presence in me; my interiority is delighted to be for you. I realize it all the more than ever before that what I do, only I can do for you. Let me join the Psalmist to say:*

Glory in His Holy Name

Rejoice O Hearts that seek the Lord!

Rely on the Mighty Lord;

Constantly seek His face (105:3, 4).

Notes:

Chapter 1
1. Patricia A McLaughlin, *The Jesus Walk* (New York/Mahwah,NJ: Paulist Press, 1997), p.5.

Chapter 2
1. Richard Rohr, *Adam's Return*, (NY: The crossword Publishing Company, 2004), p.66.
2. As quoted in Ralph Wright, *Our Daily Bread*, (New York/Mahwah, NJ: Paulist Press, 2008), p.77.
3. As quoted in Ritamary Bradley, *Praying with Julian of Norwich*, (Mystic, CT: Twenty Third Publications, 1995), p. 139.
4. As quoted in Ralph Wright, *Our Daily Bread*, (New York/Mahwah, NJ: Paulist Press, 2008), p.43.

Chapter 3
1. Albert Nolan, *Jesus Today*, (Mary knoll, NY: Orbis Books, 2007), p.146.
2. Abraham Heschael, *God in Search of Man*, (New York: Farrar, Straus and Giroux, 1955), p.83.
3. Albert Nolan, 2007, p.146.

Chapter 4
1. Thomas Keating, *Manifesting God*, (New York, NY: Lantern Books, 2005), p.94.
2. Willigis Jager, *Mysticism for Modern Times*, (Missouri: Liguori, 2006), p.72.
3. Pope Benedict XVI, *The Sacrament of Charity* (Washington, D.C: USCCB, 2007), p.71.

Chapter 5
1. Www. crossriadsinvitation .com.library_article 49.
2. Abraham Heschael, *God in Search of Man,* (NY: Farrar, Straus and Giroux, 1955), p.83.
3. www. crossroads invitation.com.library_article 49.
4. Pope Benedict XVI, *The Sacrament of Charity* (Washington, D.C: USCCB, 2007), p.34.

Chapter 6
1. Pope Benedict XVI, Jesus of Nazareth, (NY: The Doubleday Publication, 2007) p. 138.
2. Albert Nolan, Jesus Today, (Mary knoll, NY: Orbis Books, 2007), p.153.

II. My Beginning

7. I Enter into the Covenant of God

Made in God's image, we have been
endowed with the ability and opportunity
to discover our unique way of
collaborating with God in covenant
partnership.

Wilkie Au[1]

A couple met with me to set up baptism for their child. As it is the practice in our parish, I started taking down all the information of the child to be baptized. When it came to fill in the name of the church, where the parents got married, there was a silence, followed by a response and an enquiry. The response was that they got married at the beach. And the question was, "So you won't baptize the child?" My response was that we don't withhold baptism of the child because of your marriage. They were perplexed to ask, "Father what does the marriage in the church have to do with the baptism? I said, "You don't ask for baptism at the beach! Just as you seek the baptism for the child in the church you should seek marriage in the church." I took a few moments to catechize them about their own baptism. They have entered into covenant with God in the church, and for their own covenant relationship with one another they cannot afford to ignore the Church. As they left I did conclude from their body language they would consider rectifying their marriage in the church.

Biblical revelation testifies that God is the God of covenant. Pope Benedict XVI argues that the purpose of creation is the covenant: "Creation exists to be a place for the covenant that God wants to make with man. The goal of creation is the covenant, the love story of God and man."[2] God made covenant with many leading figures, like Noah (Gen 9: 8), Abraham (Gen 17:2), Moses (cf. Ex 19) at different phases of history. Each covenant was an initiative of God. Each covenant came with an indelible gift of recognizing God's presence with them. It was in and through the covenant God was making a pact with people that He is their God and they are His people: "I will take you as my own people, and you shall have me as your God" (Ex 6:7). "My dwelling shall be with them; I will be their God, and they shall be my people" (Ez 37:27). So it is God's presence in the world that would make us enter into his covenant.

Linguistic explanation of the Hebrew word for covenant, 'berith' renders the meaning of 'binding'. It binds God and man. The 'binding' begins with the people of Israel to envision the whole world in them: "All the communities of the earth shall find blessing in you" (Gen 12:3). As Pope Benedict XVI says, "Israel does not exist for itself; its election is rather a path by which God intends to come to all men."[3] All the covenants were geared to

Jesus whose presence would become a binding force to all. St. Paul offers a very lucid understanding of this binding: "And if you belong to Christ, then you are Abraham's descendant, heir according to the promise" (Gal 3:29). It is Jesus Christ who binds all of us to God.

Jesus' incarnation is the final binding force of the covenant. "Incarnation" does not just mean Jesus' birth, but Jesus' presence in the world that encompasses his life, mission, death and resurrection. Jesus' presence in the world binds each of us to God as His chosen people, going back to the very beginning of salvation history. After that of Jesus no other covenant is required for the salvation of humanity. Unlike the old covenant, which required the sacrifice of animals at the temple sanctuary, Jesus offers his own body to be sacrificed once for all. That is why the author of the letter of Hebrews says, "...He entered once for all into the sanctuary, not with the blood of goats and calves, but with His own blood, thus obtaining eternal redemption" (Heb 9: 12). Jesus' presence in the Eucharist is the lasting covenant, which is for the redemption of all.

It is at the institution of the Eucharist Jesus spelled out that it is the covenant meant for all. The words of consecration, "Of the new and everlasting covenant" and "for you and for all" aptly convey that the promise of the covenant is for all. As John F O' Grady, the Biblical Scholar puts it, " *For you (uper nous)* defines...Now all people can stand in the presence of God as daughters and sons, feeling comfortable in the presence of God as intimates knowing the love of God for all."[4] And the letter to the Hebrews has a large claim in regard to Jesus as "mediator of a new covenant" (9:15). The Presence of Jesus in the Eucharist is an exquisite mediation for all of us to have a new covenant relationship. We cherish the promise of Ezekiel that the dwelling place of God is with us by hearing the voice as heard by John: "Behold, God's dwelling is with the human race. He will dwell with them and they will be His people and God himself will be with them" (Rev 21:3). God's dwelling is the Eucharist. It is in the presence of the Eucharist, everyone enters into the covenant.

My Personal Context:

This is an amazing fact to know that I am one of the chosen ones to have the covenant relationship. It is the Eucharistic Lord who binds me to God's presence. I shall never take for granted the dwelling of God in the Eucharist because it is a promise of the covenant. I recall the early Christian prayer of the third century:

> *See, Children, what a body*
> *we have eaten, see what blood*
> *we have drunk, what a covenant*
> *we have made with our God* [5]

Meditation:

After the preparatory steps:

I am conscious of the covenant relationship that has been given to me. Whenever I receive the Lord I am strengthened in my relationship with the Lord. The covenant relationship impels me to pray: *Lord Jesus, I thank you for your presence in me; your presence in me is the fulfillment of the promise of the covenant; I am delighted to join the Psalmist to think of my parish church:*

> *I bow low toward your holy Temple*
> *I praise your name for your fidelity and love*
> *For you have exalted over all*
> *your name and your promise (138:2).*

8. I Am Baptized into God's Family

The whole being of the baptized Christian
is signed in the name of the Holy Trinity
and the mystical senses are awakened in
Him by the grace of the sacrament.

Thomas Merton[1]

It happened that during a train journey I had to travel with an Official of the Government of India. After a brief introduction of each other, he was happy to learn that I was a Catholic priest. At one point, he asked me a strange question: "I am a Hindu; you are Christian. We both believe in God. I am good; you are good. Why do you try to convert the Hindus?" Realizing within me that there is no easy answer for this question, I hesitated a bit to say, "We Christians receive Baptism, by which we are introduced into God's family and so we have the privilege of calling God "Father". We just want you to belong to God's family". He reacted right away to tell me, "Well, we, the Hindus, do belong to God's family. There is no doubt about it." I said, "How do you know that?" He said, "It is just our belief." I said, "In our case it is not just a belief; we have the Baptism, by which we know we belong to God's family." He was bewildered a bit, "what is Baptism?" I began to explain that Baptism is a sacrament and it gives to the recipient the grace to belong to God's family. He could not comprehend the word 'grace'.

It is one of many moments I realized how fortunate we are to know about the Baptismal grace that makes us children of God as compared to different religions who do not have that concept of "grace" at all.

The Prophet Jeremiah prophesized about the New Covenant that it would be inscribed in our hearts: "I will place law within them, and write it upon their hearts; I will be their God, and they shall be my people" (Jer 31:33). The old covenant was inscribed on stone tablets, and it called for a collective response and responsibility as a group. The new covenant on the other hand would be inscribed in their hearts, and so each and every one becomes uniquely responsible to experience it in his or her heart. That is why Jeremiah continued to say, "No longer will they have need to teach their friends and kinsmen how to know the Lord" (Jer 31:34). Each one would know from within how to experience God.

Among the New Testament letters, the letter to the Hebrews devotes entire chapters to the superiority and excellence of the new covenant. It was like a new sequel to the Old Covenant that helpfully expounded upon the new meaning of the Covenant to the early Christians. It deftly evinces the *interiority* of covenant relationship, compared to the *exteriority* of the Old covenant. It exemplifies the covenant relationship as "an anchor of the soul, sure and firm, which reaches to the interior behind the veil…" (Heb 6:19). In similar grand fashion, St. Paul states that this relationship is "written not on tablets of stone but on tablets that are hearts of flesh" (2 Cor 3:3). This helps us understand the sense of interiority.

The sense of interiority leads us to the sense of "indwelling." Indwelling in turn leads us to the power we have within. This power within begins with our Baptism. As Thomas Keating puts it, "The spiritual powers bestowed in Baptism are first and foremost the Divine Indwelling, which is the Trinitarian life going on within us continuously and the radical source of relationship with God."[2] This spiritual power is what we call baptismal grace that works within us. As Caroline Myss puts it, "Grace is the word we give to the power of God that we recognize in our lives."[3] Grace awakens from within us to let us know who we are for God. It awakens from within us to know what is required of us for God; it awakens within us to respond with a behavior acceptable to God. Thanks to the power of grace we have an awakening of longing for God. It is an awakening for a very personal relationship with God; it is an awakening to be with Jesus Himself. St. Paul acclaims, "Now to him who is able to accomplish far more than we ask or imagine, by the power at work within us, to him be glory in the church and in Christ Jesus to all generations, for ever and ever. Amen" (Eph 3:20).

The awakening grows ever more for the Eucharist. It is because the inward longing of the baptismal grace is drawn to an outward presence of Jesus. When we see the Eucharist the inward longing is drawn to worship Jesus. When we receive the Eucharist the inward longing is drawn to reverence the Lord. When we eat the Eucharist the inward longing is drawn to experience Jesus becoming one within us. St Ephrem makes this point in his prayer: "Lord, we have had your treasure hidden within us ever since we received baptismal grace; it grows ever richer at your sacramental table." [4]

My Personal Context:

The grace that was infused into me by Baptism directs me to the Eucharist. It connects me to the power of His presence in the Eucharist. Let me always recognize the power of His presence. Rather than approaching the Eucharistic table in routine ways, let me always be aware of the reality that grace is what draws me to Jesus.

Meditation:

After the preparatory breathing:

I am conscious of the grace within me connecting me to God. The more I realize this grace the more it becomes the power within me. Now that I am connected to God, the Eucharistic presence has strengthened me to experience this grace. I can experience this grace within me and its power impels me to be connected to God all the time. Let my prayer be this. *Lord Jesus, the grace of Your Presence within me has made me precious. Let me realize that I am with the power of Your Presence. Let me join the Psalmist to proclaim:*

> *Let the words of my mouth meet with your favor,*
> *Keep the thoughts of my heart before you,*
> *Lord, my rock and my redeemer (19:15).*

9. I Grow in Wisdom

The excellence of God's grandeur can
come to the attention of humanity through
the experience of divine power and
wisdom in human events.

Thomas Aquinas[1]

Fr.Richard LaMorte, presently the Chaplain at Marist
College, Poughkeepsie, NY at the Fortieth Anniversary of his
Ordination to the Priesthood gave out a holy card, which has his
prayer. Thanks to his permission, we have the prayer here:

Gracious God, thank you for the gift of today!

May my living today reveal your goodness.

Refreshing me, inviting me to discover your

presence in myself, in each person I meet, in each

event I encounter.

Teach me when to speak when to listen when to

ponder when to share.

In moments of challenge and decision, attune my

heart to the whispering of your wisdom.

As I undertake the ordinary and unnoticed tasks,

gift me with simple joy.

When the days go well may I rejoice!

When it goes difficult- surprise me with new possibilities!
When life is overwhelming call me to Sabbath moments restoring your peace and harmony within me. Amen.

I keep this prayer card in my breviary, and I begin the day with this prayer. This prayer helps me embark on daily life, as it encompasses everything I do each day. It makes me realize that each of us is indebted to God's Presence within us to live our lives. We *attune our heart to the whispering of His wisdom,* which is His Presence within us.

In ordinary usage, wisdom is often used to mean the ability to judge correctly. Biblical usage is much more than that. The Hebrew word *Chokmah,* for wisdom, comes from the root word *Hham,* which means *to taste* and *experience.* It connotes the personal experience. The Psalms: "Taste and see that the Lord is good" (34:9), "My soul shall taste the rich banquet of praise" (63:5) signify the experience, which is so personal. That is why, wisdom is often personified as female in order to intensify the personal character of its presence. The Book of Proverbs speaks of her: "*She* is more precious than corals, and none of your choice possessions can compare with *her*" (3:14). The Book of Sirach says, "He who loves *her* loves life; those who seek *her* out win *her* favor" (Sir 4:12). All these teachings instill in us that wisdom is personally present with a person.

The Book of Sirach describes the beginning of wisdom as "the fear of God" (1:12). Psalm 111:10 also describes, "The fear of the Lord is the beginning of wisdom." The right understanding of the word "fear" will enlighten our mind to comprehend the meaning of wisdom. 'Fear' does not refer to emotional fear; it is about the right relationship and reverence for God. Thomas Keating puts it rightly, "The 'fear of God' is a technical term in Scripture that means 'cultivate the right relationship with God.'"[2] The right relationship blossoms with the knowledge that *God is very personal so as to be present within us.* St. Luke was conscious of this "right relationship" of Father being personally present with Jesus. He mentions this twice in the same chapter in order to emphasize the fact that the wisdom was already there in the childhood of Jesus: "The child grew and became strong, filled with wisdom; and the favor of God was upon him" (Lk 2:40), "Jesus advanced in wisdom and age before God and man" (Lk 2:52). These two remarkable statements testify to the very personal presence of God in Jesus. The right relationship is the personal presence of the Father in Jesus. For Jesus, the right relationship is more than the presence of the Father in him. For Jesus, the personal presence is reciprocal: He in the Father and the Father in the Son. Jesus has confirmed this in many of his sayings. For example, Jesus said, "The words that I speak to you I do not speak on my own. The Father who dwells in me is doing his works. Believe me that I am in the Father and the Father is in me, or else, believe because of the work themselves" (Jn 14:10,11).

The reciprocal presence makes Jesus present the Father others. God is present in Jesus, and so Jesus is God's presence for others. This was evidenced in his life and message. People were so astonished at his life and message. They said, "Where did this man get such wisdom and mighty deeds?"(Mt 13:54b). Jesus knew the answer. His Father's personal presence is in him. Jesus grew with the Presence of His Father in Him. It is now St. Paul's turn to understand that Christ is the Wisdom of God (Cor 1:24). St. Paul's understanding of Wisdom as existing before all things (Wis 1:4) made him believe Christ as pre existent with God. St Paul also borrows the uniqueness of Wisdom as "first born" (Pro 8: 22) to claim Christ as "first born" (Col 1: 15). In other words, Christ is the creative presence of God. These revelations of the sacred writers guide us to understand Wisdom as the Presence of Christ.

It is in the Eucharist, Christ, the Wisdom of God, is present for us. Jesus is personally present in us. The Presence is so personal that when we receive Eucharist, we *taste* the Presence of Jesus, and we are able to *see* the Wisdom within us. The Book of Revelation invites us *to see* the Presence of God- " Behold, God's dwelling place is with the human race", and *to taste*, " a gift of life giving water"(21:3, 6). Eucharist is the life giving water, and by tasting one can truly experience personal and right relationship. That is why the practice of the catholic faith to receive 'First Holy Communion' becomes the unique moment for one to grow with His Presence, the Wisdom.

My Personal Context:

I do understand that Wisdom of God is the Presence of Christ in me. Let me also grow in Wisdom to be His Presence to others. Though I am born with the presence of God from the beginning, my First Communion made my body the tabernacle to have His Presence to be his body on earth. Let my eyes, hands, feet glorify Jesus and let me now boast in the Lord that I have grown with the Wisdom of God. Let me whisper the prayer of Pierre Teilhard de Chardin:

> *Grant, O God that when I draw near to the altar to Communicate, I may henceforth discern the infinite Perspectives hidden beneath the smallness and the Nearness of the host in which you are concealed.[3]*

Meditation:

After the preparatory steps:

I am conscious of the right relationship with God that began on the day of my Baptism. My reception of the Holy

Eucharist has intensified that relationship. I am so privileged to have the wisdom, the Presence of God in me. Let me pray: *Jesus you are the Wisdom of God in me; I grow with Your Presence; thank you for being so personal. Let me join the Psalmist to rejoice:*

> *The decree of the Lord is trustworthy*
> *Giving wisdom to the simple (19:8b).*

10. I Grow in Knowledge

Something inside of us, namely, our
attitudes about self, other people,
life and God determine all my actions and
reactions.

John Powell[1]

Christine is a young teacher of Religion in a Catholic High School. Christine is from one of those families, easily liked for their faith and dedication to God. Along with her younger sisters, when they were little, she attended Monday evening novena cum Benediction of the Blessed Sacrament. All the three sisters would recite the decade of the rosary. When they grew up, they became altar servers; they would serve at the altar with reverence and respect. Christine is also a Religion teacher, teaching in the RCIA program.

I asked her, "What made you a true Christian?" There came a spontaneous response: "My mom's influence on me: I have a vivid memory of how my mom would teach us the faith and how we should live as children of God." I intervened, "What about your dad?" She replied, "There was always a support from dad to the way mom would guide us."

"What makes you so reverential in the church?" She recalled, "As small children we looked forward to coming to church; my grandparents were a positive reinforcement in the

ways of folding my hands, kneeling, blessing myself with holy water, etc.; everything helped me to be more aware of myself in God's presence, with an automatic response of humility to pray."

"What is behind your respect towards people?" She said, *"Faith in God, and living as a child of God led me to respect others; again my parents and grandparents had a nice way of correcting us when we were disrespectful towards others."*

"What influence does the Eucharist have in your life?" She said, *"It is the personal aspect of God for me; Jesus comes into me. I feel it within me and attune myself to the prompting of the Holy Spirit."* Christine is one of thousands of youth, who grow in wisdom and understanding of who she is, who God is, and who others are in her life.

In the Old Testament the word wisdom, knowledge and understanding are used interchangeably; these words connote the same meaning at the surface reading. Yet it is good to look at the context of the text to derive its actual meaning. For instance, the Book of Proverbs says, "For the Lord gives wisdom, from his mouth come knowledge and understanding" (2:6). This text tells us that it is the wisdom that gives a person understanding. Again another text from the Book of Proverbs testifies, "Get wisdom, get understanding" (4:5). Here again, understanding is the result of wisdom in a person. Wisdom is the Presence of God that helps us gain an understanding.

St. Luke was probably mystified about the knowledge of the boy Jesus. That is why, of the four Gospel writers, he alone is interested in narrating to us the story of finding of Jesus in the temple. He cites about the reaction of the teachers to the knowledge of boy Jesus: "…. all who heard him were astounded at his understanding and his answers" (Lk 2:47). St. Luke resounds the OT understanding of *wisdom that gives one knowledge and understanding* to state that Jesus grew with wisdom, the Presence of God. That is why he writes, "The favor of God was upon him" (Lk 2:40b). So wisdom, the personal presence of God creates in a person knowledge and understanding.

What does this knowledge (understanding) do to a person? It helps the person, first and foremost to differentiate human wisdom from that of God. St. Paul speaks of human wisdom as"wisdom of this age" as that "of the rulers of this age who were passing away" (1Cor 2:8). Understanding the difference between human and divine wisdom becomes a basis for a person to understand who God is for us. By this knowledge one grows in the understanding of God and fellow human beings. It is not about grasping some theoretical ideas of God and others. It is rather a practical way of recognizing God's Presence in us and in others.

The knowledge leads us to an understanding that God's presence in us is dynamic and powerful to guide us. It creates in us awareness that God's presence is very personal. It bestows upon us the understanding of how we have become children of God. It helps us recognize that God is our Father relating to us, his children. St John says *this knowledge* helps us "to see what love the Father has bestowed on us that we may be called the children of God" (1Jn 3:1). It guides us to understand that God is present not only in us, but in all others; and so each of us is connected to God and to others. So this knowledge directs us "to love one another" (1Jn 4:11).

Jesus is the Wisdom of God present for our sake. St Paul attesting to the Presence of Christ, "in whom are hidden all the treasures of wisdom and knowledge" (Col 2:3) prays that we "share in this fullness in Him" (Col 2:10). It is in and through the Eucharist one shares the treasures of wisdom and knowledge. St. Paul brings in the institution of the Eucharist to ask, "The cup of blessing that we bless, is it not a participation in the blood of Christ? The bread we break, is it not a participation in the body of Christ?" (1Cor 10:16). St. Paul prays, "…you may be filled with the knowledge of His will through all spiritual wisdom and understanding to live in a manner worthy of the Lord, so as to be fully pleasing, in every good work bearing fruit and growing in the knowledge of God"(Col 1:10).

If we reason the teachings of St. Paul correctly, we can acquire the knowledge from the reception of Eucharist. In His presence, we grow in the knowledge of God, that is, to grow in love of God and of neighbor. We see this when we browse through the history of the church. For example, St. John Chrysostom of the third Century would say, "Give back something in exchange and do not cut yourself off from your neighbor."[2] St. Edith Stein (1891-1942) would ask, "Lord, what do you want of me?" She says, "And after quiet dialogue, I will go to that which I see as my next duty."[3] Blessed Mother Teresa of our own times would know that receiving Jesus in the Bread of Life helped her, "to serve Him in the distressing disguise of the poorest of the poor."[4] Thus we see the gift of knowledge enables us to experience the personal presence of Jesus to work in and through us.

My Personal Context:

Jesus, *The Wisdom* of God, present in me enables me to listen to St Paul who advises me to grow into the same mind that is also the mind of Jesus Christ (Phil 2:5). The Eucharist is the powerful means of God's wisdom in me, and there is no reason why I should not grow in the knowledge of God. Whenever I receive the Eucharist, I grow into the awareness of God's Presence in me. In addition to finding God within me, I must be aware of God's Presence in all I do and say. Let me begin everyday with this awareness, and at the end of the day let me ask myself: "Did I respect my mind that tells me of God's wisdom in me?" "Did I say, do and act on everything I did with God's Presence in me? "Did I respect everyone as Jesus would?" This will help me identify if I have grown in the knowledge of God and that of me and others.

Meditation:

After the preparatory steps:

I am aware of God's Presence in me. I am guided by His Wisdom. May the Eucharistic Presence in me continue to help me grow in this knowledge? Let me pray: *Lord, Just like the way You were filled and guided by the wisdom of Your Father, and just like the way You filled and guided St. Paul to have Your mind, fill me with Your Presence to grow into that same mind. Let me echo within me the Psalmist's plea:*

Teach me wisdom and knowledge,

For in your commands I trust (119:66).

11. I Grow in Healthy Dependency

As a child grows and his or her personality
develops and matures,
there develops the wonder that precisely this child,
this unique individual,
has been given to its parents.
Denis Edwards[1]

Joanne and Eric are exemplary parents, blessed with one son and a daughter: Kyle, the senior in High school and Katy a freshman. Joanne is known for her concern and love for the poor. She is one of the teachers who prepare the children for the First Communion.

Talking about her son and daughter, Joanne said, "While Kyle is intelligent and insightful, Katy is full of love and grace." This authentic affirmation of Joanne made me ask her, "Tell me something more about Katy? Why do you say she is full of love and grace?" Joanne said, "Katy has a heart set on helping others. She has a smile from God to go on a mission to help others. She went down to Mississippi to help with the continuing clean up of the Katrina disasters; she has two mission trips coming up to Mexico. I keep telling her that she is living my dreams. She is my gift and blessing."

Joanne's catholic background with her dedicated parents, John and Marion, whose extraordinary concern for others became the motivating force to her own affirmation of her own children's love and care for others. Joanne's sentiments reflect thousands of parents who continue God's purpose, which I call Parental Affectivity.

Parental Affectivity can be defined as the Spiritual force that flows through the parents to their children creating a healthy spiritual life. What primarily characterizes parental affectivity is their love of God, which is a spiritual force that activates the perfect recognition of each other as husband and wife. What the parents say and do positively affect the child and the child's response does positively affect the parents' commitment to the child. First, because it is a spiritual force it enables them to distinguish the spiritual upbringing of their children. Second, it affirms the children's life around God, Church, and the society. And so respect for God and His values becomes their primary concern and responsibility for each other. Third, it nurtures faith and morals in children. All these ways of parental affectivity are better expressed in their healthy affirmation and encouragement for their children, which paves the way for the child's healthy dependency on the parents.

God is the source of all affirmations. The origin of affirmation is God's own affirmation of creation. The author of Genesis writes about God's affirmation of the creations: "God saw how good it was" (Gen 1:12b, 18b, 25b). God's affirmation is not mere words of appreciation, but sharing of His mystical presence with creation. God's own presence in creation is the affirmation and so the creation can have the healthy dependency on God. Nothing on earth can survive or sustain without God's Presence in them. Every family on earth shares the beauty of God's affirmation and so it results in healthy dependency.

Gospel stories about the birth, infancy and the childhood events of Jesus testify to the parental affectivity and Jesus' healthy dependency. The way they presented the child in the temple (Lk 2:22) tells us of their parental respect for faith. The way Joseph and Mary took care of the child to flee from Bethlehem to Egypt (Mt 2:14) tells us of their parental responsibility. On finding Jesus at the Temple, the way that Mary questioned Jesus: "Son, why have you done this to us? Your father and I have been looking for you with great anxiety" (Lk 2:48) tell us of their anxiety and the responsibility to correct the child. All these events speak volumes about the parental affectivity.

On the part of Jesus, there manifests the healthy dependency. The way Jesus answered his parents: "Why were you looking for me? Did you not know that I must be in my Father's house?"(Lk 2:49) reveals to us of his healthy dependency. It is not a type of answering back to the parents. It is rather his recognition of the parental affectivity of Mary and Joseph. His healthy dependency inspires him to do the right thing at that time so that the parents could find him right in His Fathers house. Luke's remark about the parents-"*They did not understand what he said to them*"- tells us of the parental affectivity that enables them to have filial trust in God. The way Luke concludes the childhood narrative: Jesus "was obedient to them" (Lk 2: 51b). Obedience is the sign of healthy dependency.

Parental affectivity also has to do with the mystical effect of God's presence in them. Mary, as the mother of Jesus was "overshadowed by the power of the Most High"(Lk 1:35) to become the tabernacle of Jesus. St Luke's statement: "his mother kept all these things in her heart" (Lk 3:51) is the mystical effect of the presence of God in her. Understanding the mystical effect in the realm of parental affectivity, God's spiritual force was perfectly present in Mary that she was conscious of being the tabernacle of Jesus. The mystical effect of Mary binds Joseph and Jesus. St. Peter Eymard asks, "Can we doubt that Joseph often adored Jesus hidden in the pure tabernacle of Mary?" Joseph *adoring* Jesus in Mary is the recognition of Mary becoming the first tabernacle of the 'Eucharist.' Mary, the first tabernacle is the perfect example of parental affectivity and the healthy dependency of Jesus is the natural result of the parental affectivity of the Holy Family.

In the case of all the families, parental affectivity of the parents on the children is powerfully realized in the Eucharist.

The Eucharist characterizes the parental affectivity. The parental affectivity feeds the children; so too the Eucharist is feeding us. The parental affectivity becomes a kind of tabernacle for children; so too the Eucharistic presence invites us to come and rest. The parental affectivity animates the mutual love between the parents and children; so too the Eucharist animates the love between Jesus and us. The parental affectivity nurtures healthy dependency; so too the Eucharist fosters healthy dependency that in turn brings us ultimate dependency on God

My Personal Context:

I think of my parents, whose parental affectivity effected in me my healthy dependency. Thanks to that healthy atmosphere at home, I am healthy in all my ways. I realize each one in the family is ultimately connected to the Eucharist. It is from the Eucharist my parents are animated. It is from the Eucharistic strength they provided me with the healthy dependency.

Meditation:

After the preparatory steps:

I am conscious of the Living Presence of God, Jesus in the Eucharist. I have grown in my healthy dependency. I shall be ever more thankful to Jesus for this wonderful opportunity to grow in healthy dependency. Let me pray: *I thank you for the parental affectivity of my parents. They effected in me to grow in healthy dependency. Let me be ever connected with you now to be a person of healthy independence. Let me join the Psalmist to pray this verse constantly.*

> *Only goodness and love will pursue me*
> *All the days of my life;*
> *I will dwell in the house of the Lord*
> *for years to come (23:6).*

12. I Grow in Mature Independence

The recognition of our independence as
human beings does not diminish
our autonomy but rather springs from it.

Wilkie Au and Noreen Cannon[1]

Jaya Prakash was about 10years old, when he came to be part of the parish community of St. Joseph's parish of the diocese of Ooty, India. I was the pastor of the parish from 1987 to 1991. Jaya Prakash is from a traditional Hindu family, yet he associated himself with the church; not with the Hindu Temple. This boy was loved by all the parishioners because of his willingness to do any service at the church; he would never miss the daily mass. One time he asked me if he could be an altar server. Being a Hindu boy, I hesitated a little bit because of the regulations connected with the non- baptized at the altar. But with the permission of the bishop, we allowed him to be an altar server. Eventually he was baptized and he entered into the seminary. He was ordained a priest in 2006, and he is an excellent priest serving in one of the dioceses in North India.

Fr. Jaya Prakash belongs to the X Generation born between 1961-1981.Studies reveal that the X Generation in America was known for their intense independence to seek drastic changes that made their life meaningful. In India, on the other hand, the X Generation withdrew from the life style of previous generation to pursue rebellious ways to work to their advantage; and so, they were branded as rebels without a cause, driven not by ideals but illusions. There were exceptions.

Jaya Prakash is one such exceptional boy, born in a traditional Hindu family. He did come under the spell of the characteristics and attitudes of the X Generation. They recall the way he was drawn to serve the Lord, and the 'drastic' characteristic of the X Generation came alive in his aspiration in a very positive way to pursue his vocation. His childhood transition to say good bye to his parents at the age of 16 was a smooth one in order to enter into the seminary. His parents, though Hindus would not stand in his way to be a Catholic priest Apparently his childhood dependency on the parents was very healthy that he could grow into a mature independence. That is why he was determined to be independent of his Hindu parents to decide his own vocation to be a priest.

What is mature independence? Independence by nature is rebellious and reactive. It is healthy only when it is inner directed by self-awareness, and manifested outwardly by its holistic growth. This is what we find in Jesus' independence. Luke's citation about Jesus' answer to Mary at the finding of Jesus in the temple is a doorway to understanding his healthy independence. At the age of twelve, Jesus showed the paradigm of independence, when he asked his parents, "Why were you looking for me?" (Lk 2:49). Of course, this gives rise to the prospect of holistic growth, which entails the totality of biological, social, emotional, and psychological growth.

The holistic growth begins with the self-awareness, which makes us aware of our own inner potentials. And it makes us to be true to ourselves, to be self-determined to accomplish life's mission. These qualities of self-awareness are evidenced in Jesus' self- awareness. He was aware of his origin as the Son of God. That is why he said, "My *Father's* house." He knew his inner potentials to be a Temple Himself, which led him to ask, "Did you not know that I must be in my Father's house?" (Lk 2:49b). What is unique about his interest to be in his "Fathers house" was that it was the beginning of his self-awareness: *to belong to the Temple of God and to be a Temple Himself in the future*. And this self-awareness would unfold drastically at the cleansing of the very temple itself: "Destroy this temple and in three days I will raise it up" (Jn 2:18). This is the manifestation of Jesus' holistic growth, which began with his self-awareness at the temple.

Independence of any person is holistically mature and healthy only when it grows in reference to God. Jesus' growth of independence was absolutely in reference to His Father. That is why Luke cites, "Jesus advanced in wisdom and age and favor before God and man" (Lk 2 52). What began in the temple advanced itself in his life and mission. He knew he is God's Presence in the world. He manifested this truth profoundly in his conversation with the Samaritan woman at the well: "Believe me, woman, the hour is coming when you will worship the Father neither on this mountain nor in Jerusalem" (Jn 4:23). In this conversation 'mountain' and 'Jerusalem' refer to the 'Temple', which is Jesus himself.

'The Hour' is realized in our own times when we worship Jesus in the Eucharist. We grow in independence in reference to God's presence. The Presence of Jesus in the Eucharist is a specific invitation to each one of us to grow independent, but with God. We respond to this invitation by receiving the Eucharist into us; thereby He becomes one with us; this oneness is what is behind our mature independence; now we are all set to grow holistically in age. It is this healthy independence that makes us aware of generational conflicts that come with every age, and it is what helps us to be faithful to what we are for God till the end of our life.

My Personal Context:

Thanks to Jesus' Presence in the Eucharist, I grew in age to be independent, to have self- awareness. Henceforth, at all the transitions of different ages I am awakened to the first awareness of His Presence. In as much as I am independent in my life now, I know I am guided by Jesus' Presence within me. I am all the more delighted to say with St. Paul that "I am confident of this, that the one who began the good work in me will continue to complete it" (Phil 1: 6).

Meditation:

After the preparatory steps:

I am conscious of the dependence on my parents; I am aware of my independence to be self conscious of my affiliation to God. Let me be focused to pray: *Lord Jesus, I thank you for this beautiful awareness of Your Presence in me. At every age your presence in me brought my first awareness afresh in me that am not alone in my journey Let me bring it to completion. Let me join the Psalmist to sing of your reign in me:*

> *Your reign is a reign for all ages,*
> *your dominion for all generations*
> *The Lord is trustworthy in every word,*
> *and faithful in every work (145:13).*

13. I Grow in Interdependence.

Movements of separation that need to take place
as the child moves from total dependence through
independence to interdependent.
Ann Brennan[1]

Mark and Marisa are one of the families who are so conscious of living up to their faith. They have two daughters and a son. When the children are small, it is normally expected of the children to follow the parents in their ways of faith. They are daily communicants. The entire family is regular to the sacrament of confession. Now that the children have grown into teen age and above, the entire family is regular to the ways of faith, especially to the frequent confession. This example of the Wisniewskis made me appreciate the parental faith, which is manifested in their commitment to their ways of life.

When asked about how they brought about this commitment to themselves and their children, they attribute it to their upbringing by their own respective parents. This is a remarkable example of how parents pass on our faith from one generation to the next. Asked about the frequent confession, Marisa said about her husband's practice of reading at the dinner table some of the wonderful passages from the book, Frequent Confession by Benedict Baur. According to them, it benefited their children. Here is an example of how simple ways, such as reading at dinner table, done for a higher purpose leaves an imprint of our faith.

Marisa, a Catholic school teacher, is committed to tell the school kids, and her own children, "Faith is not something we add to our life; rather it is our life." Here is an example of how simple fact statements can make a lasting memory in the minds of the children. Parental influence is healthy for their children. Mark said, "They have grown up. They are independent. We are happy about their responsible faith and commitments. To cite an example, Mark said, "If one of them happens to be away from home on a weekend with their friends, who may not be Catholic, yet they would go for mass, even if they have to drive miles to go." Here is how a sense of healthy dependency and independence would accomplish healthy interdependence. Mark and Marisa rightly put it, "Our expectations have taken roots in them."

Children who are brought up in a healthy dependency know their parents have expectations of them, which are in perfect sync with their life pattern. Healthy dependency and mature independence are nurtured by the parental faith in God; so too their interdependence among one another is inseparably connected with God. These are the sons and daughters, who attribute their faith to that of their parents. It is evidenced in their constant approval statements, such as "my mother taught me my faith" or "my dad was a God fearing man." "My parents told me not to do this (to be unkind or to be mean) to others." This in fact brings about healthy interdependence between God and men.

What is interdependence? Basically it is interpersonal relationship, which recognizes the basic need of dependency of one another in order to grow. It also embraces the uniqueness of each one to be different from others; and yet he or she can be together with others. But the interdependency cannot be mature and healthy without a personal relationship to God. It stems from the basic truth that any human interaction without God becomes either slavish or controlling. It is the interdependence of God and man that makes man's interdependence mature and healthy.

What is the interdependence between God and man? In the context of the biblical history of our salvation, it means mutual interaction between God and man. Bernard J. Lee, an esteemed theologian, who expounding on the mutuality between God and men writes, "God, who is most real, is deeply and truly interactive…The mutuality between God and human history is real."[2] Drawing the real mutuality of God and man in the salvation history, interdependence simply means this: *on the part of God, the recognition of man needed for His plan of bringing all to perfection, and on the part of man, the readiness to respond to that recognition of God.*

We can easily comprehend the interdependence of God when we look at the creation story. The creation story testifies to the fact that interdependence begins with the initiative of God. He blessed them saying: "be fertile and multiply, fill the earth and subdue it" (Gen 1: 28). *Blessed* refers to the initiative of God and *fertile, multiply, fill* and *subdue* refer to man's responsible acts, which are intrinsically connected with the *blessed*-ness of God. When man fails to respond to God's initiative and acts in his own way, that irresponsibility causes the fall. How God had to *banish (Gen 1:23)* and to *expel (Gen 1:24)* the first parents on account of the irresponsible acts, would tell us about the fall and destruction. It is good to realize that it is the irresponsible behavior of indifference to the initiative of God that made them fall from interdependence.

To grow to perfection or to fall to destruction is the potential life story of every couple. Blessedness of interdependence is true not only for the endeavors of the couples but also those of all. God calls all men and women to be united to His Son inorder to accomplish anything on earth. Jesus all the more brings the reality of interdependence to light: "I am the Vine, you are the branches. Whoever remains in me and I in him will bear much fruit, because without me you can do nothing"(Jn 15:5). Thus the interdependence of God and men is true of every man and woman at every stage of our lives.

It is in Jesus that interdependence becomes all the more realistic. God sent His own son Jesus to create *the blessedness,* the source of mature and healthy human interdependence. Most realistically, it is in the Eucharist, interdependence becomes the source of life. Jesus himself enunciated this by saying, "Just as the living Father sent me and I have life because of the Father, so also the one who feeds on me will have life because of me"(Jn 6:57). Interdependence is nothing but God's love that initiates the healthy interaction to grow in perfection. St. John puts the whole interaction, and the effect of interdependence in a nutshell, "We love because he first loved us" (1 Jn 4: 19). This explains that the interdependence of God and man is essentially the love of God manifested in and through Jesus. So that when we interact it is Jesus who is the bond of human interdependence.

My Personal Context:

Thanks to Jesus' presence in the Eucharist, I grow in my healthy interaction with Jesus. I shall always be conscious of Jesus presence in me to respond to God's interdependence. This enables me to have a mature and healthy interaction with others I shall strive to have the mind of Jesus, and to manifest His love and action. Let St Paul's words, "So be imitators of God, as beloved children. And live in love, as Christ loved us and handed himself over for us as sacrificial offering to God for a fragrant aroma" (Eph 5:1,2). I shall never enslave others nor control others.

Meditation:

After the preparatory steps:

I am conscious of the eternal plan of God to have interdependence between God and me. I shall be ever conscious of the initiative God has taken to trust me. Let me be proud of God's trust in me to pray: *Lord Jesus, I shall never take for granted your trust in me to have come into me. It is you who should be manifested in all what I say and do. Let there be sincere interactions of my interdependence with others. Let me join the Psalmist to say:*

For you make me jubilant, LORD, by your deeds;
At the works of your hands I shout for joy (92:5).

Notes:

Chapter 7
1. Wilikie Au, *By Way of the Heart*, (NewYork/Mahwah, NJ: Paulist Press, 1989), p. 67.
2. Benedcit XVI, *The Spirit of the Liturgy*, (San Francisco: Ignatius Press, 2000), p.26.
3. Benedict XVI, *Jesus of Nazareth*, (NY: The Doubleday, 2007), p.22.
4. John F.O'Grady. *According to John*, (New York/Mahwah, NJ: Paulist Press, 1999), p.104.
5. A. Hamman, (ed.), *Early Christian Prayers*, (Chicago: Henry Regnery.Co.1961), p.140.

Chapter 8
1. Thomas Merton, *Inner Experience*, (NY: HarperCollins, 2003), p.62.
2. Thomas Keating, *Manifesting God*, (NY: Lantern Books, 2005), p.37.
3. Caroline Myss, *Entering the Castle* (New York: Free Press, 2007), p. 17.
4. *Liturgy of the Hours Vol. 3* Office of the reading for the feast of St Ephrem, June 9.

Chapter 9
1. As quoted in Mathew Fox, *Sheer Joy*, (NY: HarperCollins.1992), p.86.
2. Thomas Keating, *The better Part*, (NY: Continuum, 2005), p. 43.
3. Teilhard de Chardin, *The Divine Milieu,* (NY: HarperCollins, 1960), p.99.

Chapter 10
1. John Powel, Life giving vision, (Allen, TX: Tabor Ppublishing, 1995), p. 372.
2. As quoted in Owen Cummings, *Eucharistic Doctors,* (NewYork/Mahwah, NJ: Paulist Press, 2005), p.62.
3. As quoted in Mike Aquilina *Reflections of the Eucharist*, (OH: Servant books, 2009), p.43.
4. Ibid., p.75.

Chapter 11
1. Denis Edwards, Human Experience of God (New York/Ramsey, NJ: Paulist Press, 1983), p.31.
2. Www. childrenofhope.org/childrenadore/quotes.htu.

Chapter 12

1. Wilkie Au, and Noreen Cannon Au, *The Discerning Heart*, (New York/ Mahwah, NJ: Paulist Press, 2006), p.8.

Chapter 13

1. Janice Brewi and Anne Brennan, *Midlife Spirituality and Jungian Archetypes*. (Maine: Nichlas- Hays, Inc.1999), p.200.

2. Bernard J. Lee, *The Galilean Jewishness of Jesus*, (New York/Mahwah, NJ: Paulist Press, 1988), p.87.

III. My Call

14. I Am Endowed with God's Favor

The divine has no body on earth but yours,
no hands but yours, no feet but yours;
yours are the eyes through which the
Divine compassion is to look out to the
world; yours are the feet with which he is
to go about doing good; yours are the
hands with which he is to bless men now.

St. Teresa of Avila[1]

*Mark is 32 years old; when he was in the 11th grade, in the year1993, his English Teacher, Ms. Crosley asked him to write a paper. Mark wrote a paper titled **My evening in heaven**. Mark is the oldest of the three sons of Lou and Eilleen, who gave this paper to me to read. As I am appreciative of their parental love, faith and guidance to their children, I could understand why Mark chose this essay. Inasmuch as I would like to have the entire essay here I have to edit it for the length of the chapter.*

If I could choose anyone I wanted to spend an evening with me, I would choose someone I already know. I try to talk to him as often as I can. I see him every week and sometimes during the week also. He is with me always and I know Him pretty well. He is my God: Jesus Christ.

Jesus is my friend, but He's never been to my house! Most of my other friends have come over, but not Jesus. Sure, He's there in spirit, but He has never been physically present.

If Jesus did come over for the evening, I imagine we'd talk for a long time. We would discuss the events of 2000 years ago when Jesus was alive on Earth. How He taught the people, performed miracles, and how He suffered and died. He thought of each one of us individually while He hung on that cross, and that is why each of us is called to eternal happiness with Him in Heaven. I would have the opportunity to thank Him, face to face.

I would ask Him about the condition of the world today. We'd discuss the corruption and evil that happens in the world while most people sit back and watch.

We would pray together for all the sinners like myself. We would also pray for the poor, for the sick. We would pray for people with serious problems-people who do not have jobs, food, clothing and shelter

I would think that my life would dramatically change after we met face to face. I guess I would be asked to sacrifice a lot personally. It would be worthwhile, though, just to meet Jesus to know that someday, I would be praising Him forever in heaven.

No wonder his teacher rated this 'wonderful'. Reading this essay after almost 20 years, and knowing Mark now as an intelligent, sensible and caring person, I wonder if this essay is something more than an English essay. Probably, he had no clue at the age of 16, why he was conscious of these thoughts about his relationship to Jesus. But we know that it was the favor of God, which was upon him, but not necessarily known to the young mind. Luke says about boy Jesus at the age of twelve that "the favor of God was upon him" (Lk 2:52).

What is the Favor of God? Favor is not about favoritism, as it has no place with God. The Hebrew word for favor is *Hen* comes from the root *Henan*, which means to bestow or to show grace, or to show favor to some one. It is also the root word for *Chen*, which is grace; That is why 'favor' and 'grace' are used interchangeably in the OT and in the NT. What is so dynamic about, *hen or chen* is that the recipient of that favor will be dynamic to be something for others. When God bestows the favor, it animates a dynamic activity in and through the person. Dynamic activity comes about because an intimate love of God is shown to the person concerned. The remarkable passage in the Book of Exodus, testifies to this intimacy: Moses said to the Lord, "You have said, 'you are my intimate friend,' and also, 'you have found favor with me.' Now, if I have found favor with you, do let me know your ways so that, in knowing you, I may continue to find favor with you" (33:12, 13). Moses is receptive to God's favor, and that made him a man for others. To be receptive to God's favor makes him dynamic on behalf of God for others. The New Testament begins with the story of Mary, where the Angel Gabriel hailed Mary saying, "Hail, full of grace", which is also translated as "Hail, favored one" The Angel also reiterated, "You have found favor with God" (Lk 1:30). Like Moses, Mary too was receptive to His favor, and the whole world experienced salvation through her receptivity.

For St. Paul, the dynamic activity of God is none but Jesus Christ himself. He knew the Hebrew language, and knew the dynamic meaning of both favor and grace, and so he wanted to tell us that the favor and grace can only come through Jesus Christ. So He translates the dynamic activity of God in Greek by the word *Charis*. He thanked God for people who found favor with God, "I give thanks to God always on your account for the grace of God bestowed on you in Jesus Christ" (1Cor 1:4, Eph 1:6). He testifies to the dynamic activity of God as he himself was a favored one: "By the Grace of God I am what I am, and his grace to me has not been ineffective" (1Cor 15:10). So the favor of God in Jesus qualified St. Paul to be a dynamic Apostle.

All of us are favored children of God. St. John puts it, " See what love the father has bestowed (favored) on us that we may be called the children of God. Yet so we are"(1Jn 3:1). Eucharistic Presence *favors* all of us, as each of us is an intimate child of God. Each of us should be receptive to His grace, and so the dynamic activity continues in this world through each of us. That is why St. John says, "whoever acknowledges that Jesus is the Son of God, God remains in him and he in God" (1Jn 4:15). Thereby each of us can be His hands, eyes and feet to go about doing good.

My Personal Context:

I am the favored one for God. The Eucharistic Presence fills me with His favor. Whenever I receive the Eucharist, I should be receptive to His dynamic activity in me, so that I become His hands, His feet and His eyes. As Pierre Teilhard de Chardin said each of us can become Jesus' Body for others, and that "we will bring to Christ a little fulfillment."[2]

Meditation:

After the preparatory steps:

I am conscious in me of the intimacy by which Jesus has favored me as His body. Let me be concerned about other's difficulties, and let me be good to others in need. The intimacy by which he has favored me impels me to pray: *Lord You have favored me. You have bestowed me with grace upon grace. I am receptive to Your favor. May I be Your body to do good for others. Let me join the Psalmist:*

> *Remember me, Lord, as you favor your people*
> *Come to me with you saving help*
> *That I may see the prosperity of your chosen,*
> *rejoice in the joy of your people*
> *and glory with your heritage(106:4,5).*

15. I Was Introduced to Others

We ourselves cannot know the
depths of our own goodness and giftedness
until someone else first loves us and calls
these things out of us.

John Powell[1]

It all happened in a Jesuit boarding school in India. I was in sixth grade. In the 1960's, it was a custom that all the boarding schools run by the Jesuits had a Spiritual Director for the boys. I had a Spiritual Director, a saintly priest, Rev Ambrose Gnanadicam. His holy life still resonates in my mind, as it was the source and force for all the boys in their studies and careers.

It happened one day, after the choir practice conducted by Fr. Ambrose, as we were coming out of the church. My dad was waiting for me to visit me. Fr. Ambrose was conversing with my dad, and said something, which perplexed me then. He said to my Dad, "Your son is a good boy; he will make a good priest." There was something unique in the way he introduced the goodness in many of us. At that age of twelve, for the first time to hear such a significant prediction from such a holy priest, it seemed so natural for me to think of myself a priest right away. It fostered such a response from me that I never shied away from making a statement like "I want to be a priest." All through my high school years, nothing ever distracted me from such a focus.

After almost 33 years of my priesthood, I know that it was Fr. Ambrose who truly introduced me to my Call.

Our culture tends to judge people at face value. But among close relations, we may go beyond face value to understand loved ones before we judge them. In the case of Jesus and John the Baptist, we know they are cousins. Yet in the Gospel of John, we are told that John says, "I did not know him…" (Jn 1:31). While it is true they were cousins, we cannot imagine that the cousins did not know each other. In all probability it took years for John to know that Jesus was more than a cousin, and to know him as "a man existing before me." He was inspired by God to know Jesus, and to introduce him to others.

Introducing is an act of genuine acknowledgement of someone's goodness and giftedness, and of making it known to others. It does not happen by coincidence or by chance. It is God's Presence that motivates one to see others' goodness and giftedness. John testifies to this by saying, "the one who sent me" made him see who Jesus truly was.

There are people who have low self-esteem and others who have healthy self-esteem. Those with healthy self-esteem are the ones who can indirectly act on behalf of God to go beyond the face value to appreciate the goodness and the giftedness of others. And, those with healthy self-esteem are the ones who are genuinely humble to listen to God in order to acknowledge others' goodness. As Caroline Myss puts it, "Humility allows you to recognize and acknowledge all the positive qualities of body, mind, and spirit in another person."[2] It is evident from John's introduction of Jesus: "He must increase; I must decrease" (Jn 3:30).

And when he came to know Jesus, he could not wait to let the world know about Jesus. Again his humility is seen in going into the wilderness, preaching and practicing repentance. After all these humble preparations, he finally introduced Jesus as the Lamb of God. It seemed as if he could not wait for that day to accomplish the introduction. He said, "Now I have seen and testified that he is Son of God" (Jn 1:34). Biblical scholars may say that John *pointed out* Jesus to others. In the context of what we have seen in John's experience, I want to say John *introduced* Jesus to others.

St. Paul, attesting to Jesus' humility wanted the Philippians, to learn from Jesus' example. "Do nothing out of selfishness or out of vain glory; rather, humbly regard others as more important than yourselves, each looking out not for his own interests, but the interests of others. Have among yourselves the same attitude that is also yours in Jesus Christ" (Phil 2: 3-5). Jesus emptying Himself became the Lord, and so the entire world is connected to Him, and kneels before Him in worship

(Phil 2:10,11). This is the most obvious reference of how Jesus' emptying becomes the Eucharist to the worshiping community. Jesus' act of emptying reached its climax when He Himself became the Bread to be broken. 'Emptying' and 'Bread broken' embody themselves in the Eucharist, which becomes the life and summit of our daily life.

Pope Benedict XVI describes, "Worshiping the Body of Christ means believing that in that piece of Bread there really is Christ, who gives meaning to life, the immense universe and the whole human history as well as the shortest existence."[3] And so, at the heart of every Catholic, there is an experience of union with Eucharist. This union has resulted in many appreciating the goodness and the giftedness of others in our life. Let me allow the words of the late Pope John Paul II, ring in my heart: "From the Eucharist comes the strength to live the Christian life and zeal to share that life with others."[4]

My Personal Context:

It is an awesome experience for me to come across so many people who are so inspired to have the humility to appreciate the goodness of others. Thanks to the Eucharist, this experience still continues. I gratefully remember all those who have the humility to appreciate me, and to introduce me to others. It has helped me grow. Let me marvel at the emptying of Jesus to be present for us in the Bread. In the words of St. Francis of

Assisi: "What wonderful Majesty! What stupendous Condescension! O Sublime Humility! That the Lord of the whole universe, God and the Son of God, should humble Himself like this under the form of a little bread for our salvation."[5] Let the Eucharist encompass me to grow to see the goodness and giftedness of others, and to introduce others in my life.

Meditation:

After the preparatory steps:

I am conscious of my relationship to Jesus. Just as Jesus sent others to appreciate me to make me grow, let me also empty myself in such a way to be there for others. Whenever I meet someone who needs to be introduced to others, let me gladly do so. Let me pray: *Lord Jesus. I am grateful to you for your humble Presence in the Eucharist. Your humility was there to appreciate me, and to make me grow .I am also thankful to many men and women who were moved by your Presence to appreciate the goodness in me. Let me join the Psalmist to proclaim:*

> *I will praise you always*
> *For what you have done*
> *I will proclaim before the faithful*
> *That your name is good (52:11).*

16. I Was Guided to My Call

Between myself and men, and with the
help of your eucharist, you want the
foundational attraction to be made
manifest-that which mystically transforms
the myriad of rational creatures into a sort
of single monad in you, Jesus Christ.

Teilhard De Chardin[1]

For some, it is a matter of astonishment when they come to know about my two priest- brothers. In India it is not uncommon among Catholic families to have more than one son or daughter who have accepted the call of the Lord to religious life. When people ask me the reason for this blessing in our family, I credit it to my parents, and especially to my mom, whose pious and exemplary life inspired us to heed the call. With her presence, each of us was so attuned to look for directions to listen to the call of the Lord.

Fr. Andrew Selvaraj happened to be our pastor where we grew up. We were altar servers. I am the oldest of my two priest brothers. Fr. Bellarmine is a Salesian priest, who recalls the beginning of his vocation in the context of Fr. Andrew's words of appreciation. Bellarmine, who was affectionately called 'Bella' was told by Fr. Andrew, "Bella, I see the simplicity of Fr. Thomas, your uncle in you. If you become a priest, you will be a simple priest like him." Fr. Thomas, my maternal uncle is known for his saintly life; he passed away in 1982.

Bellarmine became interested in the call to be a priest. Then it was the turn of my paternal uncle, Fr. Martin, who encouraged him to join the Salesian Apostolic School as an aspirant, at the end of his eighth grade.

Psychologists affirm that every child has a legitimate need to be respected, noticed, affirmed, and admired of their potential to develop. What happens to the one who is noticed and respected of his or her potential? When the children's potentials are admired and affirmed, they are helped to notice their own values. They grow in self-esteem, which is about their sense of the values which others notice in them, and whether they stand up to them. In the words of Pierre Teilhard de Chardin, the foundational attraction created by the Eucharist is made manifest in the affirmation of those wonderful values. It is not only the child who is in need of legitimate affirmation, but also the adult life is in need of it.

This self-esteem is behind many choices we make in our lives. It is a fact that our choices are shaped by the constant affirmation we receive from our communities. It is usually others' presence and direction that help us know the goodness of ourselves. It is the kind, and encouraging words of others that touch us to grow, even to the extent of responding to the call of the Lord. Someone said that almost 40 percent of our values remain within us dormant and they go useless (used less) to the grave. It is because others who noticed our values neither respected them nor expressed them.

The Creation story has the remarkable admiration of God for the creation: "How good it was"(Gen 1:10,12,18,21,25). The admiration was meant to bless man to find his own goodness of power, "to be fertile and multiply; to fill the earth and subdue it" (Gen 1:28). This became a base for all of us, as the very image of God, to admire and bless others. We see the admiration of God blessing the prophets, though they were hesitant to accept themselves. For example, Isaiah said he had unclean lips; but the Lord's admiration for him made him clean to be a prophet (Is 6:5). Jeremiah said he was too young and did not know how to speak; yet God's admiration for him made him a prophet(Jer 1:4).

Jesus' words of admiration to Simon, "You will be called Kephas" (Jn 1:42) brought out his leadership potential to be the leader of the Apostles. Jesus' words of admiration to Nathanael, "Here is a true Israelite. There is no duplicity in him" (Jn 1:47) made him the Apostle Barthalomew. Jesus' way of noticing, respecting, admiring others was something very spontaneous in his interaction which is so evident from the Gospel narratives. This is what brought so many people to listen to him, and to follow him. Psychological understanding about Jesus' life and ministry emphasizes the effective role of positive affirmation that is associated with ones growth and ministry. Jesus himself could not perform any mighty deed because of the lack of faith (Mk 6:5). People did not want to affirm the potential power of Jesus, and so Jesus could not do mighty deeds among them. His own instruction to his disciples, "whatever town you enter and they do not receive you" (Lk 10:10), underscores the affirmation needed for the effective ministry.

Experiencing the Presence of Jesus in their life, the first Christians lived up to their call to encourage each other. It is evident from St. Paul's words and ministry. He would affirm their values, saying for instance, "We are his handiwork, created in Jesus Christ for the good works that God has prepared in advance, that we should live in them"(Eph 2:10). He would associate himself with them by encouraging words: "It is right that I should think this way about all of you, because I hold you in my heart" (Phil 1:7). He would always instruct them to affirm the values of others, "Encourage one another and build one another up, as indeed you do"(1 Thes 5:11).We should heed to St. Paul's plea:" Humbly regard others more important than yourselves, each looking not out for his own interests, but also everyone for those of others"(Phil.2:3b, 4).

God purposed the Eucharistic Presence as the foundational attraction to be an everlasting affirmation for all of us. It is in and through his Presence that God has affirmed and accepted us. It is in and through His Presence that others have been affirmed to help us grow. It is in and through His Presence that we have grown to embrace our call. It is in and through His presence that we grow in the choice of our career.

My Personal Context:

I think of all those wonderful people, whom the Eucharistic Presence affirmed to be part of my choice of call or career. Beginning with my parents, my priests, my friends, and my guides have been sent by the Eucharistic Presence to affirm my self –esteem. Again, with the Eucharistic presence I have grown into what I am today. They saw me with that potential and with their encouragement I have grown.

Meditation:

After the preparatory steps:

The Presence of Jesus sent me all these wonderful people; they have influenced my call. Thanks to the Presence of Jesus in the Eucharist, they were guided to influence my call. It is with the sense of profound joy I celebrate His presence, the very source of encouragement. Let me pray: *Lord, let me acknowledge your Presence that encourages me all the time. Make me be an instrument of encouragement for others. I shall join the Psalmist to cherish your own affirmation for me:*

You are the most handsome of men;
fair speech has graced your lips,
for God has blessed you forever(45:3).

17. I Was Introduced to Him (Her)

You may live perfectly ordinary life in the
world, but your interior life is anything but
ordinary. You continue your external life,
but on the inside you are awakened,
fearless, conscious, a resource for others.

Caroline Myss[1]

Michael and Jessica were married in St.Mary's Church on June 28ᵗʰ.of 2008. I consider it a privilege to have done the paper work for their wedding, and to have married them. It is because of that simple fact that I was able to see something beyond the ordinary in each of them as they prepared themselves for their wedding. I was interested in knowing what was that "something beyond the ordinary" in them.

As they were aspiring to be teachers, they met each other at the prep-period. It started with a kind of joking, but inviting attention to each other. Jessica would joke about Michael's habit of eating a pop-tart and Michael would joke about Jessica's expensive way of using the marker pencils. Though in hindsight it was ordinary joking they said they had experienced a liking towards each other to date further. Both of them could see the Hand of God in it.

Jessica thanked God when she came to know that Michael is Catholic. In fact, that bond of being Catholics brought them to church every Sunday. They would sit right in the first pew. When asked why they preferred the first pew to other pews, they said they wanted to remain focused, and to participate rather than be spectators of the Eucharistic celebration. Again this may seem ordinary, yet they were awakened to the Presence of God.

Michael recalled his younger days of going to different churches since one of his parents belonged to a denomination other than the Catholic Church. Going to church was just a ritual, but he felt his experience at the Eucharistic Celebration was more realistic. So he resolved to go through the RCIA program to be a Catholic. He determined that his children would not have to go through the plight of going to a different church, and to miss the Eucharistic celebration. He was delighted at the fact he was to marry Jessica, a Catholic.

During their dating, they were faithful about praying together; they were so accustomed to saying, "Bless us O Lord, and these thy gifts..." to say grace together before meals. This may seem ordinary, but it is more than an ordinary means to remain faithful to the Lord. Through their ordinary life they were introduced to each other, to be for each other for the rest of their life.

In the Old Testament, people had an experience of God's closeness to them in all they said and did. So much so, that the OT history itself in their understanding, was not the record of human events, but that of God's experience with them. People knew that God was at work to accomplish His purpose in everything they did: "I say that my plan shall stand. I accomplish my every purpose" (Is 46:10b).God would accomplish His purpose in what they *said*: " Man may make his plans in his heart, but what the tongue utters is from the LORD"(Proverbs 16:1). God would accomplish His purpose by guiding their steps: "In his mind man plans his course, but the LORD directs his steps"(Proverbs:16:9).Those who trusted these ways of God, prayed relentlessly for His help all the times in their life: "My help comes from the LORD, the maker of heaven and earth....The Lord will guard my coming and going both now and for ever"(Ps 121:2;8).When they were not sure of the right way, they would pray: "to see if my way is crooked, then lead me in the ancient paths"(Ps 135:24). "You guide me along the right path for the sake your name" (Ps 23:3).

Jesus himself, knowing the OT tradition of the people, continued teaching, "Your heavenly Father knows all that you need. But seek first the kingdom of God, and His righteousness, and all these things will be given you besides" (Mt 6: 32, 33). The *Kingdom of God* is His presence, and *the righteousness* is understood as God's Plan and Purpose in ordinary life. God's presence is His closeness to us. The Mystic, Meister Eckhart, who believes in God's presence as a force flowing through our ordinary life, says, "God is closer to me than I am to myself; my being depends upon God's being near me and present to me."[2] God's closeness to us is to unfold His plans for us.

Jesus Himself becomes God's Presence in the Eucharist to be at work with the believers: "For the Bread of God is that which comes down from heaven and gives life to the world" (Jn 6:33). Pope Benedict in his post –synodal Apostolic exhortation, encourages the people, "They should cultivate a desire that the Eucharist have an ever deeper effect on their daily lives, making them convincing witnesses in the work place and in society at large...."[3] The deeper effect comes about even when we know His closeness to us. As Basil Pennington puts it, "Jesus walks into our daily lives in many ways- sometimes invited, sometimes not; sometimes welcome and sometimes not so welcome. But he always comes, the bearer of the good news."[4] To be awakened to Jesus' closeness is the key to experience His guidance all the time.

My Personal Context:

My life has been guided by His purpose at all times. In all I have said and done, I realize the LORD has been part of my life. In the OT, sometimes people did not comprehend the ways of the LORD. They even verbalized it saying, "Behind and before you encircle me and rest your hand upon me. Such *knowledge is beyond me, too lofty for me to reach"* (Ps 139: 5, 6). I see the

Eucharistic Presence so tangible before my eyes, and I will always take to heart the exhortations of Pope Benedict: *"There is nothing authentically human-our thoughts and affections, our words and actions- that does not find in the sacrament of the Eucharist the form it needs to be lived to the full."*[5]

Meditation:

After the preparatory breathing:

I am conscious of Jesus within me. He has guided me from my birth in all my words and actions. He has been part of me ever since I received the Eucharist. He has been guiding me in my ordinary life. He introduced me to her (him). He has been part of my life. Let me pray: *O Lord Jesus, I am grateful to you for being within me. You have been at work within me, even when I was not conscious of your Presence in me. Let me surrender my life completely to your Presence and guidance. Let me sing with the Psalmist:*

> *You are my hope, Lord;*
> *my trust, God, from my youth.*
> *On you I depend since my birth;*
> *From my mother's womb you are my strength;*
> *my hope in you never wavers (71:5,6).*

Notes:

Chapter 14
1. St. Theresa's quote from www. Quotecatholic.com
2. Pierre Teilhard de Chardin. *The divine Milieu* (NY: HarperCollins, 1960), p.26.

Chapter15
1. John Powell, *The Christian Vision*, (Allen, TX: Argus communications, 1984) p.62.
2. Carloine Myss, *Entering the Castle*, (NY: Free Press, 2007), p.112.
3. Pope Benedict XI quoted from the homily at the John Lateran on the Solemnity of Corpus Domini, 2008.
4. Pope John Paul II in his address to the Bishops in India.
5. St. Francis of Assisi's quote from www.quotecatholic.com/Francis of Assisi.

Chapter 16
1.Pierre de Chardin, *the Divine Milieu, (*NY: HarperCollins, 1960), p.122.

Chapter 17
1. Caroline Myss, *Entering the Castle*, (NY: Free Press, 2007), p.78.
2. Meister Eckhart as quoted in Albert Nolan *Jesus Today* (NY: Orbis books, 2006), p.143.
3. Pope Benedict XI, *The Sacrament of Charity*, (USCCB Publication, #7, 2007), p. 67.
4. Basil Pennington, *Seeking His Mind*, (MS: Brewster, Paraclete Press, 2002), p.33.
5. Pope Benedict XI, 2002, p.60.

IV. My Preparation

18. I Transition from Insecurity to Security

> Our emotional programs based on the
> instinctual needs of the child have found
> their true home: God is our security, God
> is our Beloved, and God is our freedom.
>
> Thomas Keating[1]

A few years back, a couple came to me at the Diocesan Family Counseling Center in Ooty, India. To safeguard their anonymity, let me name them Roy and Rose. They came to me as almost a last recourse to their mindset for separation and divorce. Although divorce is very rare in India, some of the counseling centers are rather active with many couples' problems.

Roy had been married to Rose for almost eight years when they met me. He was emotionally abusive to her and at times physical abuse was the means of giving vent to his anger. After probing into his life, especially into his childhood, I could ascertain his remembrance of his drunkard father, and his childhood haunted by insecurities created by him.

Having I learned about the studies of Thomas Keating about energy centers, and the emotional programs of childhood, I tried to situate behavioral problems of Roy with that understanding. After a few sessions of counseling, Roy came to the realization of how he had repressed those painful emotions, and he responded readily to dismantle those unconscious insecurities. As a man of faith, willing to go through a few meditation techniques, he was able to change his ways to connect with others, especially with his wife. It did not come as a surprise for me to know that the couple is living happily thereafter.

According to Thomas Keating, all of us are in need of Self-knowledge, which entails an insight into *the emotional programs of the three energy centers*: Survival/Security, Affection/Esteem, and Power/Control. Early childhood develops primarily by the gratification of the instinctual needs, such as need for emotional bonding, belonging, caring feeding etc.. Most likely, everyone has had moments, when the needs were frustrated by some unhealthy way or other. These frustrated moments thereafter sought false ways for happiness to meet the needs connected with survival, affection and power. As a child no one was conscious of how these instinctual needs were met. From the first years until we became conscious, the brain acted like a computer recording our emotional responses to these instinctual needs. The human brain saves these 'memory files.' These false ways are known as 'programs' saved as 'files' in our brain. Thomas Keating calls these false ways *emotional programs*. These emotional programs continue to influence us to find happiness in a false way. As conscious as we are, we have to have the self-knowledge to dismantle them in order to lead an authentic life.

Self-knowledge is about how these emotional programs of energy centers have been influencing our feelings and actions. For example, the first energy center of Survival/Security is in need of food, drink and breath at the right time, place and by the right people. When these are not there, the child develops insecurity, and the pain associated with that is repressed in the unconscious of the child. We call this *false self,* which would create weakness of will to influence wrong motivations and actions. It can be set right only when we develop self-knowledge, and the conscious self-purification. Self purification is a sort of soul searching with the help of God's presence in us to dismantle the negative cravings of the emotional programs of the energy centers.

Jesus, having grown in age and wisdom, was all set to inaugurate his ministry to establish the kingdom of God. Jesus did not have the false self, nor was there any need of dismantling it. Yet he wanted to envisage his ministry according to the plan of God, that is, to do all for God's glory, and not for his personal glory. So he took up a journey into the desert, which in Psycho-spirituality is to have a *desert experience.* The desert is a dry place with an environment lacking water and greenery. So too we humans go through a sort of stressful dryness, which necessarily longs for a place of solitude and divine experience. The desert experience is also understood as an experience of solitude in preparation to launch into action for God. Jesus was not under stress, but he wanted to have this experience of solitude in preparation for his ministry.

The temptation story of Jesus, according to the Gospel accounts, is remarkable in the context of the energy centers. The first temptation was to rekindle the self-knowledge, which consisted in tackling the first energy center of survival/security. Jesus knew much more than we know now about food, water and breath. He thinks of the crooked ways and the short cuts of the false self of the worldly standard (devil) to turn the stone into bread to satisfy that energy. He counteracted it with a profound realization: "One does not live by bread alone, but by every word that comes forth from the mouth of God." This realization would lead him to say to his disciples, "My food is to do the will of the one who sent me and to finish his work" (Jn 4:34).

His self realization was manifested in Him to be the Living Bread and the Living Water: "I am the living Bread of life (Jn.6:35), "Whoever drinks this water I shall give will never thirst again" (Jn.4:14). His own self realization would caution the people about the cravings of the false self: "Do not work for food that perishes, but for the food that endures for eternal life, which the Son of Man will give you" (Jn 6:27). What the Son of Man would give is His own body, the Bread of life: "My flesh is true food, and my Blood is true drink" (Jn 6:55). Thus we see the eternal connection established between the first energy center and the Eucharist.

My Personal Context:

I am conscious of my false self. I am in need of dismantling the insecurities of my emotional program. Unlike Jesus, my emotional programs have been afflicted in many ways. I have buried within me the acts of shame, humiliation, discouragement, grief, fear, anger, and anxiety. I know I have covered these up all my life under the guise of false self, which is known only to me and to God. Now, with Jesus' Presence in me, I shall lead myself to the desert experience of self-knowledge, and I shall take time to be alone in the Presence of Jesus, and to be genuine to scrutinize my childhood, and its impact on all what I have said and done.

Meditation:

After the preparatory steps:

I am conscious of the Presence of Jesus in me as my Security, my Beloved, and my Freedom. As the Living God in me, He knows my first energy center. He knows the way my false self has been influencing me all these years. Let me take up the courage with His Presence to go through all what I know about my childhood. Let me now ask the Lord to dismantle my false self and its ways. Let me straighten up my ways from now on and for this I pray: *Lord Jesus, I have breathed into me your Breath. I thank you for the self- knowledge you have created in me. It is not too late to change my false motivations and ways in my life. Let me be aware of you as my Living Bread and the Living Water all the time in my life. Let me sing with the Psalmist to thank the Lord:*

> *I was hard pressed and falling,*
> *But the Lord came to my help.*
> *The LORD, my strength, and might,*
> *came to me as savior(118:13,14).*

19. I Transition from Low Self-esteem to Self Affirmation

Behind manifest grandiosity there
constantly lurks depression, and behind a
depressive mood there often hides an
unconscious (or conscious but split off)
sense of a tragic history.

Alice Miller[1]

A young priest, ordained at the age of 27, now four years a priest, was in two parishes serving as the Associate Pastor. I met him a few times during these four years. He looked depressed every time I met him. Whenever I asked him, "How are you?" he would say "Good." Although he said 'Good', he did not mean it. Added to this, I noticed in his constant verbalization of discontent: "No one appreciates me. It is a thankless job." One does not have to be a psychologist to understand that he has low self-esteem, which craves constant appreciation from others to keep going. Thomas Keating's studies of energy centers, and emotional programs, would say that his second energy center has been largely affected.

The second energy center is about Affection and Esteem. When a child is deprived of emotional needs of attention, appreciation and admiration, he/she could suffer the tragic loss of self-esteem. Self-esteem is based on one's own authentic forms of affirming one's goodness, and not based on certain qualities we possess. These qualities are most likely the projections of compensatory means for the frustration at various stages of the loss of affection and esteem of our childhood. Thomas Keating defines one of those compensatory means as Performance Orientation (PO). "Performance" here does not refer to the service we do, but the ulterior motives, like striving for approval and appreciation that propel us to do that service. The opposite of PO is Love Orientation (LO), which is an authentic service without looking for any appreciation or recognition. Whether there is recognition or not, we do what we do out of a sense of service.

PO usually puts up 'grandiose' performance. It is a kind of showy element, such as words and acts just to get applause or appreciation. If it does not result in getting the appreciation at the end of the performance, one feels depressed. Their verbalization invariably comes out saying, "No one appreciates me." "There is not a single person there to thank me." These are indications of PO in a person, and how he or she is prone to depression.

The second temptation of Jesus is about the second energy center of affection and esteem. His desert experience was a means to weigh the difference between authenticity and hypocrisy. He was prepared to deny himself any grandiose nature of seeking vainglory. This is evidenced from the temptation when he was asked to demonstrate a jump from the parapet of the temple to get assistance from the angels. Jesus was asked to seek that vainglory to win the admiration and love of all. Jesus' reply was He would not allow himself to be persuaded by the test: "You shall not put the Lord, your God to the test" (Mt 4: 7). This self-affirmation was to insinuate a mindset to challenge anything that would come in his way to serve and not to be served: "Son of man did not come to be served but to serve and to give his life as a ransom for many" (Mt 20: 28). The only motive that would impel him to serve was the love for the mission that His Father gave him to do.

Jesus all through his ministry was conscious of the remarks of the Prophet Isaiah: "Since this people draws near with words only, and honors me with their lips alone, though their hearts are far from me, and their reverence for me has become routine observance of the precepts of men"(Is 29: 13). Jesus would recall these remarks of Isaiah to tell the Pharisees and scribes of their performance orientation (Mt 15: 8). About grandiose performance, He said, "Take care not to perform righteous deeds in order that people may see them"(Mt 6:1), "When you give alms, do not let your left hand know what your right hand is doing…"(Mt 6:3). About striving hard for appreciation, He said, "When you have done all you have been commanded, say 'We are unprofitable servants; we have done what we were obliged to do" (Lk 17:10). Without seeking undue recognition and appreciation we should be prepared to do our service.

Finally, the service of Jesus reached its magnitude of renunciation when He offered his own Body on the cross. Now with his own Body he purposed to be present at the Eucharist to continue to be of service to the whole of mankind. He continues to be the sign of renunciation and strength to get rid of the false self in each of us. Jesus' presence in the Eucharist is the power to create in us this self-knowledge, by which we can dismantle our false self.

Thomas Keating writes, "God knows us through and through and does not impose upon us more self knowledge than we can handle at anyone point in our spiritual journey. However, as we become more humble and let go of our need for compensatory activities, the Inner Light that results in deeper knowledge increases."[2] Eucharistic presence is the source of inner power that sheds light into us. We should be humble to allow Jesus to help us grow in self-knowledge, and to let go of compensatory activities. Eucharist alone can make someone genuine to be at the service of others.

My Personal Context:

I can understand why those moments of 'grandiose' performance were part of my life. Now I can realize that I was looking for undue appreciation from others. I am conscious of a few things wrong with my second energy center. The Lord knows about all that did not go well with my childhood, and all that influenced my performance orientation. Now that Jesus is within me, my life should be in the words of Karl Rahner: "to be good to someone from whom there is no sign of appreciation or gratitude, or renouncing something without receiving recognition from others or even feeling inward satisfaction,…" [3] From now on, I come to my self-knowledge to act with my true self. I shall look up to the Eucharist, and let the Lord in the Eucharist be my strength.

Meditation:

After the preparatory steps:

I am conscious of the Lord in the Eucharist guiding me to accept myself as I am, without any pretension. With His presence in me, I have realized my performance orientation. And so let me pray, *Lord Jesus, Thank you for freeing me from performance orientation, and restoring my true self. Help me, Lord to be true to myself. I shall join the Psalmist to pray:*

> *Guide me in the truth and teach me,*
> *For you are God my Savior (24:5a).*

20. I Transition from Control to Love

> The more that you experience Gods steady,
> reliable love, the less likely you are to turn to
> controlling others to secure positive feelings
> about yourself.
>
> John J. Cecero[1]

At one of the family sessions for the married couple in India, I had to lead the couple to the understanding of the three energy centers of Survival/Security, Affection/Esteem, and Power/control as advocated by Thomas Keating. At the end of every session, some time was devoted to question and answer. There was a question that made all the ladies burst into laughter. The question was: "Why are the husbands so controlling of their wives?" I pointed out to her that it was okay to use the 'pontificating plural' to include all wives in her question; otherwise it would sound as if her husband was controlling her.

In the context of India, almost all the marriages are arranged marriages. Women pay a dowry. Many women find it very difficult to accept the irony of being controlled by men despite the dowry brought into the family. It is not rare to see families struggle with this issue of the controlling attitude of the husbands. So, the question was rightly fitting in the context of many families.

My answer amounted to explaining childhood needs, especially in the area of the third energy center of Control/Power: Dysfunctional families frustrate the early childhood in unhealthy ways, such as being overly strict, finding fault all the time, punishing with physical abuse etc. Unfortunately these ways create in children excessive guilt, which in turn makes them withdraw from life with forms of self destructive, self blaming habits, or makes them aggressive to dominate others, and in many other ways of over identification. At the end of this explanation, I remember to this day the lady remarking humorously, "So they are sick!" I could see the group had a reason for laughing.

The third temptation of Jesus was about the third energy center of power/control, and its emotional program. With the desert experience, Jesus resolves that no craving for power/control would hamper him from doing his mission. He emerged victorious with a heightened self-awareness and determination of his ways that it would never be used to control or to have power over others. The False self demanded him to 'prostrate', so as to make him succumb to the power of the kingdom and its magnificence. His self-affirmation led him to say, "The Lord, your God, shall you worship and him alone shall you serve" (Mt 4:10). It means Jesus was determined to honor His Father alone in him, and not the world and its magnificence.

Unlike Jesus, the false self dictates us to control and to dominate others. Contemporary psychology has confirmed that children who have suffered frustration in their early childhood tend to have an obsession to control three areas: place, things and persons. There is a legitimate need to have a decent place to live, or to have the necessary things to use, and to exercise power over others in the context of job or work. The cultural conditioning makes it perfectly normal to have these legitimate needs, but, in the case of those who are afflicted with painful memories, according to Thomas Keating, they may disguise them unconsciously to have over identification of cultural conditioning. *Over identification* is a compensatory way to make up for the childhood frustration. It is done by over identifying oneself with ones own family, gender, group, place, things, and persons to the extent of detrimental disrespect or control of others. They identify themselves in an aggressive way with ethnic groups of castes, nationalism, racism etc.

Jesus defined over-identification with the remarkable statement: "Where your treasure is, there also will your heart be" (Lk 12: 34). His genuine concern about over-identification was also detailed in asking, "What profit is there for one to gain the whole world yet lose or forfeit himself?" (Lk 9:25). This entailed his disciples to renounce any sort of *attachment to places, things and persons.* Regarding the over-identification with place, Jesus was determined to tell them, "Foxes have dens and birds of the sky have nests, but the Son of Man has nowhere to rest his head" (Lk 9:58). Regarding over identification with things, Jesus shocked his followers when he told the rich man, "Go, sell what you have, and give to the poor...then follow me" (Mk 10: 21). Regarding over identification with the persons, Jesus' renunciation did not even spare his own family His self-affirmation was such that he would not over-identify himself with his own family for the sake of the global family: "Who are my mother and brothers...Here are my mother and my brothers. For whoever does the will of God are my mother, brother and sister" (Mt 3:33-35). He expected of his disciples the same mind: "Whoever loves father or mother more than me is not worthy of me, and whoever loves his son or daughter is not worthy of me" (Mt 10: 37). Jesus wanted his disciples to give up places, things and persons to be at the service of every one.

About the sense of authority, Jesus summoned his disciples, "You know that the rulers of the Gentiles lord it over them, and the great ones make their authority over them felt"(Mt 20:25). He warned them of qualities of Pharisaism, that is, inviting attention to their power and presence in all they say and do: "all their works are performed to be seen….. "They love places of honor"… "Seats of honor" (Mt 23:5,6). Jesus forbade them the titles of 'Master' or 'Rabbi,' because those titles were associated with a sense of superiority and pride (Mt 23: 7-10). He exhorted them to humble themselves. And at the Last Supper, just before he instituted His Presence in the Eucharist, His words reached the action of humility in washing the feet: "You call me 'teacher' and 'master,' and rightly so, for indeed I am. If I therefore, the master and teacher, have washed your feet, you ought to wash one another's feet" (Jn 13: 13,14). Thus Eucharist has become the everlasting reminder of the renunciation of the false self.

My Personal Context:

Jesus is my model for renouncing the cultural conditioning of over identification. St. Paul realizing the supreme good of knowing Jesus considered everything as rubbish to gain Christ (Phil 3: 8). In the Eucharist, I see the perfect humility of Jesus, "who, though in the form of God…emptied himself, taking the form a slave" (Phil 2: 7). But Jesus has become the power to bestow all I need. Now I can present myself to His Presence to get rid of all the emotional needs, which have been clamoring in me to have control and power over others.

Meditation:

After the preparatory steps:

I am now conscious of my presence to His Presence in the Eucharist. Without any excuse or false justification of cultural conditioning, let me reject my cravings of power and control. Let me pray: *Lord Jesus, I have now witnessed your Eucharistic Power to heal me of all my unnecessary needs of power and control. Your humility on the cross has paved the way for me to surrender my power to you. May your presence in me be my power and strength. Let me join the Psalmist to pray:*

> *Probe me, God, know my heart;*
> *Try me, know my concerns (139:23).*

21. I Fulfill God's Purpose in Me

Fullness there, fullness here, from fullness,
fullness proceeds. Once fullness has
proceeded from fullness, fullness remains.

Indian liturgical prayer[1]

The Blessed Sacrament Monastery of the Sacramentines sisters is in Scarsdale, New York. I had the privilege to visit the monastery. These sisters are dedicated to perpetual adoration. It was a joy to celebrate Eucharist for them. After the Eucharist, I expressed my eagerness to meet with anyone of the sisters to learn more about their experience of Eucharistic adoration. The community happily pointed out the Superior to fulfill the task.

Sister Mary Veronica, the Superior of the community, was gracious to answer some of my queries about her experiences. I asked her, "What do you truly think of the religious call which is only devoted to Eucharistic adoration?" There came a spontaneous reply: "It is a great blessing." The congruence between her words and the bodily cues, especially the facial cues, revealed the authenticity of her response. Joyful as I was to have come to know a true response, I was enthused to listen to her experience.

Sharing the experience of her presence in front of the Blessed Sacrament, she said that it is like a knock at the door. She recalled the reference from the Book of Revelation:

"Behold. I stand at the door and knock. If anyone hears my voice and opens the door, I will enter his house and dine with him and he with me" (Rev: 3:20). She emphasized, "The knock is from within me." The 'Within'-experience is always a sign of fullness, which necessitates the person's response. She said that her life and her devotion to the Eucharist is an experience of love. In my 15 minutes of listening, I could count at least twenty times the word 'love,' referring to her worship of the Eucharist. The word 'love' used many times in the context of her call to perpetual adoration of the Eucharist is a sign of the sense of fulfillment of the religious life.

The concept of fullness derives its meaning from the Greek root word *pleroo,* which refers to *that which fills.* It is a matter of abundance and completion. The concept of fulfillment is more of a Hebrew usage. The Hebrew words, such as *Male, Kala, Qum* convey the meaning of completion of time and events, which necessitates a new beginning towards the fullness. The Hebrew and the Greek concepts are evidenced in Jesus. At every stage of His life, when something was fulfilled, something new of God's purpose would unfold. We see the unity of time and events. For example, Jesus beginning (time) his ministry (event) was meant to unfold God's purpose for people to experience God in Him.

Jesus began the ministry after the desert experience, as explained in the previous chapter. While Matthew and Mark give the details of the temptation story, Luke skips the details of it, probably, to draw the attention of the readers to the *beginning* of the ministry. According to Luke, the beginning of Jesus' ministry was a fulfillment, toward a new beginning for people leading to fullness. So, Luke records, "This is a time of fulfillment" (Lk 1:15). Having gone through the soul-searching of the three energy centers (survival/security, esteem/affection, power/control) as part of the desert experience, Jesus is all set to begin his ministry to lead all to the fullness of the kingdom of God.

St. Paul grasps the concept of fullness of Jesus being fulfilled at fullness of times. It was God's plan "to set forth in him as a plan for the fullness of times, to sum up all things in Christ, in heaven and on earth" (Eph 1:10). He proclaimed that the believers "share in this fullness in him, who is the head of every principality and power" (Col 2:10). And so, St. Paul encouraged everyone, as sharers of God's fullness in Jesus, to see that we fulfill the ministry that we received in the Lord (Col 4:14). So, by sharing in the fullness of Jesus, each of us has to fulfill God's purpose at every stage of our life. The time of baptism, the time of reconciliation, the time of First Eucharist and Confirmation are all the stages of our life. These stages of fulfillment are not to be taken as a demand of law, but stages leading us towards the fullness of love.

Institution of the Eucharist is the fulfillment of God's purpose for us to receive the grace which guides us to the fullness. St. John's words testify to it. "And the Word became flesh and made his dwelling among us…From His fullness we have all received, grace in place of grace"(Jn 1:14,16). It is in the Eucharist that we receive the fullness of 'grace in place of grace.' What is *grace in place of grace*? Scripture Scholar Bernard Lee presents the Eucharist to argue convincingly, "It is not that we have to become something we are not, but that we have to allow God to complete in us what God has already begun in us."[2] In Jesus we have already received the fullness to be God's own people. When we receive the Eucharist, we are not becoming something we are not. It is Jesus, who continues His Presence of fullness in us, guides us towards the fullness of eternal life.

My Personal Context:

At the time of my baptism, I received the fullness of grace to belong to God's family. That was a fulfillment, which was a beginning and progression of a new life. When I received my First Communion, there was a sense of fulfillment in receiving the Body and Blood of Jesus, yet another time of fulfillment came to be when at Confirmation I received the fullness of Jesus' Spirit. These stages coincide with the stages of biological growth which is also the fulfillment of God's purpose in me. Now that I have grown into the beginning of adulthood let me revere these stages of life as a fulfillment towards the fullness of life. Having come to this realization, let me give a sublime determination to the fullness of life Jesus is offering to me in the Eucharist: "Unless you eat the flesh of the Son of Man and drink his blood you have no life within you"(Jn 6:53). The Eucharistic Presence in me certainly leads me towards the fullness of eternal life (Jn 6:54).

Meditation:

After the preparatory steps:

I am conscious of Jesus, who resides in me offering the fullness of life from within me. I have gone through all these unique moments of fulfillment of Jesus' Presence in me. Now I am all the more delighted to experience within me that fullness that continues to lead me to the fullness of life eternal. And so let me pray: *Lord Jesus, I am thankful to the fullness of time I experienced when you came into me; and today is yet the fullness of time for me to experience you within me as the fullness of life. Guide me more and more to this moment of fulfillment and fullness. Let me offer you my fitting praise by joining the Psalmist:*

You will show me the path to life,
abounding in Joy in your presence
the delights at your right hand for ever (16:11).

22. I Experience Kingdom of God within Me

The man whose view of life is purely secular hates himself
interiorly, while seeming to love himself. He hates himself
in the sense that he cannot stand to be "with" or "by"
himself. And because he hates himself, he also tends to hate
God, because he cannot abide the inner loneliness which
must be suffered and accepted before God can be found.

Thomas Merton[1]

*Some years back, there was a Graduation mass of the
eighth graders of a Catholic School in one of our churches in
New York. I was one of the concelebrants at the mass. The Pastor
who presided over the mass gave out the awards, and asked them
to keep up the faith, that should be a guiding factor in their
future. Before dispersing, he did an excellent job of
congratulating the students, thanking the parents, above all,
thanking God for the gift of Catholic education. All these did not
matter anything to two of the kids, who graduated. No sooner
they were out of the Church, than we saw them changing their
shirts with T-shirts, which read, 'I have survived catholic school'.*

Some of the parishioners, who noticed the kids' behavior
with those T-shirts, were outraged. Many of them had some good
lines to say about the kids. One of them remarked, "This is the
impact of a secular culture; I am only sorry for these kids". While
some younger minds are a prey to be swept away easily by the

current of secularism, there are also other minds that take their catholic education seriously. While, some think of this as a trend of the teen age's fancy rebellion to the values, some may brush it off as nothing. But it is the sign of secularization, with an imminent danger of unrest that people have, while seeming to have fun. The contemporary world with its mania of secularization constantly perpetuates the three 'temptations' in many forms. To put it concretely in the words of Pope Benedict XVI, "Secularization with its inherent emphasis on individualism has its most negative effects on individuals who are isolated and lack sense of belonging."[2] The victims of secularization hate themselves, and so they hate any value of God and His Church.

Jesus, at the beginning of His ministry, asked the people 'to repent' right away (Mk 1:15). Repentance is the translation of Greek word, metanoia. Contemporary Christian understanding of metanoia refers to contrition and conversion. The classical Greek meaning of metanoia, before the Christian understanding, was *to have an after thought to change ones mind or heart about someone or something.* Mark writing the Gospel in Greek, used the word, metanoia, which is the translation of the Hebrew word Teshuvah, which means *return*. Teshuvah is the OT process of returning. It encompasses first one's own realization of sins that broke the covenant between him and God, and then coming back to God with acts of fasting, wearing sackcloth, and offerings at the temple. Therefore, metanoia is the process of transformation that entails changing of ones ways so as to return to God. In the context of the secularism, one is asked to change his ways of secularism and return to God and His values.

Jesus went on to say that the *Kingdom of God* is within you. What has repentance to do with the kingdom of God in the saying of Jesus? Kingdom of God is not a geographical location with boundaries. The people of Israel had a narrow vision of the kingdom with the expectation of the Messiah for their king redeeming the people from the foreign power of the Romans. Jesus, the Messiah, began his ministry by proclaiming the coming of the kingdom. It is as if he was saying, 'You look for a king and the kingdom; in my presence you have the kingdom of God. So change your ways of looking for a kingdom' (cf. Lk 17:21), and start returning to me. My presence is the kingdom; from now on, let your life be transformed by my presence." Jesus, in identifying the kingdom of God with Himself was certainly consistent with many other ways (cf. Mt 7:21, Lk 13:20, Mk 4:26).

What does *within* mean? The Greek word *entos* is translated within, or among or in the midst of. Hebrew equivalent of *entos* is *quereb*, which means *inside*. In the context of Jesus' proclamation of the kingdom, and the meaning of repentance, we can definitely say that Jesus meant that the kingdom of God is *within* you. It is the Presence of Jesus in the midst of people that made it possible for them to have a *within* experience.

When we look at the Eucharistic presence, we look at Jesus, who asks for the same within experience. It is *with* His presence, we have His *within* presence in us. There is a challenge that comes with His presence. We are asked *to repent*, because there is need to change the secular ways, by which we have been looking at things and persons. Christ's Presence in the Eucharist proclaims the need to challenge this trend of secular lives.

Repentance in the Eucharistic Presence leads us to an interior transformation which is a radical experience. It is radical because it changes our life from within. As we have seen, the Kingdom of God is Christ's Presence in the world, and anyone who has the repentance experience will have the Kingdom of God within him. As Michael Roden says, "In effect, the kingdom of God becomes everything to the individual who finds. It turns ones value system upside down as it changes ones life."[3] Thus all of us can experience His Presence in us.

My Personal Context:

Thanks to the Presence of Christ in the Eucharist, I experience the power of conversion. My old ways that were under the spell of secularism have opened my self to His Presence in me. Whenever I receive the Eucharist, the union God has established within me is being confirmed and strengthened.

What the great saint, St Leo the Great has said about the Eucharistic transformation has become true in me. I shall recall his words: "The leaven of our former malice is thrown out, and a new creature is filled and inebriated with the Lord himself. For the effect of our sharing in the body and blood of Christ is to change us into what we receive. As we have died with him, and we have been buried and raised to life with him, so we bear him within us, both in body and in spirit, in everything we do."[4]

Meditation:

After the preparatory steps:

I realize now my new ways in which I live for God. Let me thank God for the experience of repentance; let me thank God for His presence in me. Let me continue my *within* experience all the more. Let me pray: *Lord I am so delighted that I have found the kingdom of God within me. Your presence in me is what I count on when I am challenged by the secular world. Let me therefore join the Psalmist to say:*

> *Therefore my heart is glad, my soul rejoices;*
> *my body also dwell secure(16:9).*

Notes:
Chapter 18
1. Thomas Keating, *Manifesting God,* (NY: Lantern Books, 2005), p.106.
Chapter 19
1. Alice Miller, *Drama of the gifted Child*, (NY: Perennial, HarperCollins, 1997), p. 33.
 2. Thomas Keating, *Manifesting God,* (NY: Lantern Books, 2005), p. 100.
3. As quoted in James A Wiseman, *Spirituality and Mysticism*, (NY: Orbis Books, Mary knoll, 2006), p.156.
Chapter 20
1. John J Cecerro, *Praying through our life traps*, (NJ: Resurrection Press, 2002), p. 76.
Chapter. 21
1. www.concentric.net~cosmos/bede_griffiths_pooja.htm
2. Bernard Lee(Ed) *Alternative Futures forWorship, TheEucharist.Vol.3.* (Collegeville, Minnesota: The liturgical Press, 1987), p. 51.
Chapter 22
1. Thomas Merton, *The Inner Experience*, (NY: HarperCollins, 2003), p. 54.
2. Pope Benedict XI, The Sacrament of Charity,(USCCB Publication,#7,2007),p.65
3. Michael Roden, *A church not made with hands*, (VA: Hampton Roads, 2005), p. 57.
4. Cf. Sermon by St Leo the Great, *(Liturgy of hour, II Vol)*.p. 661

V. My Community

23. *I Nourish Communion with My Family*

We all belong to many human communities,
but none touches us so deeply as the family.

Elizabeth A.Dreyer[1]

Leo is an extraordinary person whose generosity has helped four girls to study nursing. Thanks to him, Pravi, Cathy, Dyana and Fatima are nurses in India. Without the generous help of Leo, these girls from poor economic backgrounds would never even dream of studying nursing, as they could not afford to pay the tuition. One time, I thanked Leo for this extraordinary help for which he gave me an answer, which edified me. He said, " My wife Jeanne who passed away in 1990 was a nurse. One of my daughters, Marguerite, is now a nurse practitioner. I am happy to help these poor girls to be nurses." Leo's reminiscences of the family vocation made me think of the family 'communion' that becomes a 'charitable communion' to others in the human family.

Leo's sentiments about nursing are a remarkable source that helped the girls. "Jeanne was a very caring person to the sick. This is one profession," Leo said, "that cares for the sick." This moved me so much that I had to instruct the girls about the nobility of this profession. They assured me of their gratitude to

Leo by keeping up the sacredness of this profession. What makes Leo happy is that the four girls refer to Leo as "Uncle Leo!" I explained to Leo the Indian culture of respect and reverence, why someone calls another "uncle." It is a cultural form of addressing those who are so kind and generous to them. Though they are not part of the family, those who address them consider them as loving as an "uncle" to them. Leo's experience of communion with one another in his family is extended to be part of communion of another family elsewhere in the world.

Jesus' proclamation of the Kingdom of God gives rise to human community and communion. Commun-ion (ity) comes from the Greek word *koinonia*, which connotes the intensity of mutual relationship between two or more persons. In the New Testament, the idea of koinonia is understood as fellowship, which is rooted in divine communion. Though Koinonia is the New Testament word, it drew its essential meaning from the origin of divine communion as revealed in the Book of Genesis.

God revealed Himself in creation and made the family as His image of communion: "God created man in his image; in the divine image he created him; male and female he created them. God blessed them, saying: Be fertile and multiply; fill the earth and subdue it" (Gen 1:27,28b). The communion between husband and wife in a family is the design of God. And so every bond that exists between husband and wife, father and mother, brothers and sisters, parents and children in Family becomes the reflection of the divine communion between the Father and Son and Holy Spirit.

Jesus himself used the image of family to proclaim his own relationship as that of Father and Son. In accepting Jesus, we become the brothers and sisters of the family of God. In the remarkable context where Jesus said, "Here are my mother and my brothers" (Mt 12:49), Jesus celebrated the very insight that all of us are brothers and sisters of God's family. Jesus had a perfect communion between his foster father, Joseph and mother Mary. That is the reason why it is known as the holy family. It is because of this perfect communion, Jesus was able to extend the same image of family relationship to all who followed him.

We see the progress of human communion of the holy family surrounding the close relatives in Jesus' ministry. It is seen with his own cousin John who would baptize him. His own near relatives- as mentioned as 'brothers and sisters' (Mt 13:55, 56)- are associated with his ministry (Mk 3:31, Jn 2:12). His own near relatives, like John, James, and Jude were his disciples. In and through Jesus, the divine communion was experienced in the proximity of the families. So much so, the first disciples went about calling their own kith and kin to follow Jesus. Traditionally, Andrew and John were the first disciples who followed Jesus (Jn 1: 37). Andrew brought his brother Simon to

Jesus (Jn 1: 42). John is supposedly to have brought his brother James to Jesus. So in Jesus one finds his union so dynamic he cannot but share that communion with others in his family. This was the experience of Jesus' disciples. Their divine communion in Jesus made them share that communion with their loved ones in their families.

St. Paul proclaimed that we are the children of God through Jesus Christ: "For through faith you are children of God in Christ" (Gal 3: 26). And so he described the church in the image of the family. He sees in the relationship between husband and wife, the symbolic relationship between Christ and His church. That is why Paul addressed the followers of Christ with the metaphor of family bond and relationship. He addressed them as 'children' (Eph 5:1), 'brothers' (2 Cor 13:11, Col 1:1,2) and 'sisters' (Rom 16:1, Phlm 1:2).

Ultimately it is Christ's presence that made us all brothers and sisters of God's family. In our contemporary times, beyond the family we are used to calling others as brothers and sisters. But it is the Christian experience of God that called us to address others as brothers and sisters. Mostly because Jesus is the Son of God, we, as His brothers and sisters, belong to the Family of God. And we are called to address each other as brothers and sisters. The Eucharistic Presence of Jesus surrounds us all the time. So each and every family is united in Him to make us all one family.

St. Peter Julian Eymard exclaims so well, "The Eucharist is the link that binds the Christian family together. Take away the Eucharist and you have no brotherliness left."[2] The Eucharistic Presence of the Lord is behind every help, generosity, and support we give to the other. And it is the Eucharistic Presence of the Lord that makes us belong to one family beyond the narrow circle of ones own family.

My Personal Context:

It is understandable to me why we have been calling the Eucharist communion. It is because I have communion with God in Jesus. Primarily it is my family that enjoys communion in the Eucharist. I shall take care that this fellowship first binds my family and me. I should assume the responsibility to be an example in all what I say and do. If necessary, I should walk extra miles for the sake of others to help others.

Meditation:

After the preparatory steps:

I have breathed into me the power of the fellowship of God. Communion with the Eucharist brings into me the blessing of fellowship with each one of us in the family. Let me pray: *O Lord, I thank you for giving me the fellowship. Strengthen me never to leave this fellowship, and help me always to be a witness to this communion. Let this begin with me and with my family members. All along let me sing with the Psalmist:*

> *All the families of nations*
> *will bow low before you (22:28b).*

24. I Nurture Communion with Others

> There is considerable significance in the
> fact that the bread that is eaten is broken
> and yet from one loaf. We are drawn into
> the *koinonia* that is the life of the Trinity.
> Its extension into history is *diakonia*.
>
> John C.Haughey[1]

A few of the Eucharistic Ministers serving in the parish of St Mary's, Wappingers Falls, are delegated by the Pastor to take communion to the homebound. Everyone does it with the sense of service. Of all of the Eucharistic ministers, one couple, namely, Mike and Jane are delegated by the Pastor to coordinate the availability of some of the Eucharistic Ministers, and reach out to the homebound and the sick on a regular basis. For the past 25 years, this group has been active taking communion to the sick and the homebound. Jane in particular is very enthusiastic to take communion to the sick. Jane and Mike themselves could number almost a thousand visits of bringing communion.

Asked about what motivated the couple to volunteer to such an extraordinary service, Jane replied that God's presence within her has been the source of grace, which motivated her to take up this service. She considers this service as a way to be close to Jesus. Asked about her own health problem, with the surgery on her hip, she said that her husband would jump in to do the service in such difficult moments. Both of them see this service as loving sacrifice to go beyond themselves to care for others.

What is more commendable is that when they are asked, they oblige to take the Eucharist to hospitals. Thus, the time and energy they put at the disposal of God's children is a witness to what is known as diakonia

(A few weeks before the publication of this book, Jane passed away, and now shares the Eternal Eucharist)

When Jesus inaugurated the kingdom of God, He made it very clear to the people that the kingdom is meant for all. In the case of the earthly kingdom, only those who are in that territory would be eligible to enjoy that kingdom. God's kingdom- as we have already seen in the previous chapters- is the Presence of God, bringing about the communion. This kingdom reaches everyone regardless of nation, class, color and creed. It includes all. We have witnessed the progress of this kingdom reaching out with the genuine concern for all and the inclusion of all towards their communion and their salvation. The Kingdom of God, according to Pope Benedict XVI, is "over the world and over history, transcends the moment, indeed transcends and reaches beyond the whole of history. Its inner dynamism carries history beyond itself."[2] So, the Kingdom of God is the Lordship of God with an inner dynamism and the Lordship of God is the Lordship of God in Christ: The inner dynamism of the Lordship of Christ is practically experienced with the communion of all.

Communion of God, manifested by Jesus, began to take roots in all the people, and they were impelled by it to share with others because all who came to Jesus recognized His Lordship. And the dynamism of the Lordship of Christ was moving them to act in his name, and to receive others. The teaching of Jesus, "whoever receives you receives me, and whoever receives me receives the one who sent me" (Mt 10:40) was a guiding force to experience God in and through Jesus, and to share with all. And the dynamism of Jesus was to go beyond oneself, and "to do for one of these least brothers of mine" (Mt 25:40) was in their mind to serve others. The move to serve others was to move out from his place: "Let us go on to the nearby villages that I may preach there also. For this purpose have I come" (Mk.1: 38). Thus we can understand the dynamism of Jesus, which was the force behind his communion with his disciples. The dynamism of Jesus was seen in his teaching to recognize every one's need and to serve them.

The same dynamism of communion existed in St. Paul. His concern for others to experience communion with Jesus is consistent in his preaching and in his missionary journeys. For instance, in his writing he would refer to, "God of all, who is over all and through all in all" (Eph 4:6). For St Paul, communion of the individuals with Christ and in Christ created the community, which he calls 'Body of Christ': "Now you are Christ's body, and individually parts of it" (1 Cor 12:27). St. Paul's description of the notion of body tells us of how each individual is so connected with the other to care for this body. This caring is born out of the communion we have with each other. And so this caring is what diokonia is all about.

The Eucharist is and will be the reality of Christ's Body. It is not just a symbol, but the reality of making us one Body of Christ. St. Paul encouraged all to participate in the communion of the Eucharist. He asked, "The cup of blessing that we bless, is it not a participation in the blood of Christ? The Bread we break, is it not a participation in the Body of Christ? Because the loaf of bread is one, we though many are one body, for we all partake of the one loaf" (1Cor 10:16,17).

St. John sees the continuation of this earthly participation in the heavenly worship. His vision brings to us the glimpse of the universal participation, where new hymn is sung in praise of the same participation. "They sang a new hymn: Worthy are you to receive the scroll and to break open its seals, for you were slain and with your blood you (Lord) purchased for God those from every tribe and tongue people and nation"(Rev 5: 9). So, Eucharist is an experience that continues into a heavenly worship.

It is all the more reason why diokonia is profoundly elevated in its service.

My Personal Context:

I am conscious of my own participation when I receive communion. It strengthens me to have larger communion with others; to go beyond myself, to reach out to others without any bias or prejudice. I shall take responsibility to be something for all. Let me be an example in all what I say and do. Let me never justify anyone being left out on account of the race or color or nationality.

Meditation:

After the preparatory steps:

I have breathed into me the power of communion of God Let me create in my mind that beautiful imagery that all of us are made into one Body of Christ. Let my heart always feel for others to nurture that communion of God with others. Let me pray: *O Lord, strengthen me to be an instrument of communion to all. Act in me so that I may manifest your goodness to all to nurture this communion: Help me to join the Psalmist to sing about our journey of all the nations into the heavenly liturgy:*

> *All the nations you have made shall come*
> *To bow before you, Lord*
> *And give honor to your name (86:9).*

25. I Grow with Compassion for the Sick

Suffering wears a thousand faces, and
every face is Christ's. When we suffer
sickness, loss, or violence, or the harsher
effects of aging in ourselves or those we
love, we cannot really understand the
reasons, but we can choose the rock on
which to stand.

Genevieve Glen[1]

Ray and Louise are one of our excellent couples, known for their devotion to the Eucharist. They are daily communicants. Everyday Ray would set up for the first mass, which is at 7 AM, and assist the priest at the mass. He was a Lector and a Eucharistic minister. He did all these services for about 45 years. Now they are home bound they long to receive Holy Eucharist. I visit them with the Eucharist daily except weekends.

Ray has developed Parkinson disease. Louise and the whole family have been so exemplary in caring for him. He has no complaints. Rather he is so gracious to accept it. When asked about how he could be so gracious, he says it is God's love which has prompted him to accept it. He says Eucharist has been always his strength and will be his strength till the end. And he says, "When God calls me I am ready to go".

Louise has a witnessing mind. She says God has been wonderful to them. She remembers the Gospel quote: "Much

157

will be required of the person entrusted with much" (Lk 12.48). It is significant to listen to the way Louise understands this quote. She admits, "While it is human to complain sometimes, I feel God has entrusted us with much faith, and so, much is demanded of us to suffer illness." It is remarkable to see the way they accept the illness and offer it up for them and for others. Another significant thing is the way both are concerned about others' health. When they come to know about someone who is ill, they are moved with compassion for them. Their response is always this: "Please tell them that I send my angels to them." This is evidently compassionate concern. In spite of their illness, they also have concern for others.

(Between writing this chapter and the publication of the book, Louise passed away. May she give angelic assistance from heaven!)

Jesus began his ministry with extraordinary concern and care for others. Who are these others? During the time of Jesus, the social culture categorized them into four groups: the sick, the poor, women, and children. These were the most vulnerable 'others', who were considered the last and the least in the social order. They were culturally outcasts, religiously cursed, and politically sidelined. Jesus introduced a new direction of the social order. His priority of concern and care not only reached these unfortunate ones, but also considered them as his own. His concern was not merely *sympathy*, by which one shows his/her supportive words and at times was accompanied by acts of kindness. His concern was not merely *empathy*, by which people tend to go an extra mile with others to show their solidarity. Jesus' concern was one of compassion.

Compassion is the fruit of His mystical union with the Father. Jesus Himself testified to it by saying, "The Father who dwells in me is doing his works" (Jn 14:10b). It is this mystical union-'Dwelling in me'-that unites Jesus to us with Him and with His Father. Without this union, every one is just an individual, deserving just sympathy or empathy. With this union, every one is one in Jesus, and so every one is respected as His own. All deserve compassion, which is more than sympathy or empathy.

Let us take the concern of Jesus for the sick. We can infer from the Gospels that the priority of Jesus' kingdom was to show compassion to the sick. This depth of compassion can be understood when we study the Greek word, *Splagchnizomai*. This Greek word is the translation of the Hebrew word *racham*, which means the deepest feeling of God for His people. *Splagchnizomai* expresses the deepest yearning of emotion, which stirs the bowels, which may have a negative connotation in today's usage. But 'bowels' for the Greek is the seat of love, kindness, pity etc. Knowing about the sickness that affects another person stirs one's bowel to have pity on that person. For example, we read in Matthew's Gospel, "His heart was moved with pity (compassion) for them, and he cured their sick" (Mt 14:14). In this context, 'moved with pity' is the compassion. It is the vigorous action, preceded by the knowledge that sickness is evil. That knowledge stirs the deepest emotion, and Jesus heals the person.

Eucharist is an on going presence of Jesus at work to heal the sick. It is the compassionate presence of Jesus. Jesus is moved with pity to reach out to the sick. Jesus was outrageous about the suffering of the sick, because it is evil in the sight of God. It stirs the bowels to move into action. Sickness is not the will of God to be accepted. If sickness is God's will, there is no point in God healing it. God wants to heal it in and through Jesus' Presence. Those of us who are connected with Jesus in the Eucharist are moved with pity for others. The compassion of Jesus should be our compassion for others who are sick. In our own contemporary times we have witnessed Mother Theresa' life; for her the compassion is *"to be the living expression of God's Kindness: Kindness in your face, Kindness in your eyes, Kindness in your smile."*

My Personal Context:

When I am sick, I know it is not God's will. God is not happy about my sickness. I can see why Jesus continues His

160

Presence in the Eucharist. He wants to be compassionate towards me and to heal me. Let the compassion of Jesus make me compassionate towards others. As Dali Lama says, "Compassion is the true sign of inner strength." Let me be in touch with the Eucharist to have the inner strength that moves me to respond to the suffering of the sick.

Meditation:

After the preparatory steps:

Jesus has come into me. His compassion makes me grow into His compassion for others. Let me never ignore the sufferings of others that are sick. Jesus' presence in me makes my compassion His compassion. Let my concern be genuine as that of Jesus. Let it proceed from within me to respond to the needs of the sick. Let me make a difference in a world that contends only with sympathy or empathy. Let me pray: *Lord let my concern be more vigorous than just the words of sympathy or empathy. I desire your compassion to reach out through me to the sick. Help me to have Your Presence as the power of compassion for others. Let me keep in mind and heart of the words of the Psalmist:*

> *As a father has compassion on his children,*
> *So the LORD has compassion on the faithful (103:13).*

26. I Grow in Compassion for the Poor

Made and sustained as the Body of Christ through the
Eucharist, the community of the church takes seriously
the practical social and moral obligations flowing
directly from this sacrament. The sick, the poor and the
marginal in the community are assisted.

Owen F. Cummings[1]

About four years back, a couple, Ed and Kathi, from our parish came up with a decision to set apart weekly charity to the poor. Besides contributing to the parish church every week, they decided to give 50 dollars weekly to be sent to poor families in India. They have helped the medical needs of the poor, and helped five students to complete high school studies. Another couple, Bob and Ginny decided to help one of the Tsunami victims in India. They set apart $ 200 every month to educate a girl from a Tsunami hit family. Bob and Ginny are so happy to know that the girl, whom they helped, is now an engineer.

One time I asked Ed and Kathi what impelled them to do such an extraordinary charity. They did not want me to take it as extraordinary. Rather, they verbalized their conviction, saying, "God has blessed us, and we are happy to share it with the unfortunate. We are happy it helps someone across this country in India." Bob and Ginny said, "It was heartbreaking to see the devastation of the Tsunami. Here in this country we are so fortunate in many ways. And so we decided to help at least one family hit by that tragedy"

According to Think Quest's facts, figures and statistics, about one third of the world is fed well, one third is under fed, and one third is hungry and starving. Over five hundred million people in Asian, African and Latin American countries are living in what the World Bank has called "absolute poverty." Another fact is hard to believe, but true of America, that one out of every eight children under the age of twelve in the US goes to bed hungry every night. While these are some of the terrible pictures of the world's poverty, unequal distribution of wealth is what is most troubling to anyone who thinks right. Think Quest reports, "nearly one in four people, 1:3 billion-majority of humanity live on less than $1 per day, while the world's 358 billionaires have assets exceeding the combined annual incomes of countries with 45 percentage of the world's people."

The families mentioned above are two of many families who are conscious of the reality of the unequal distribution of wealth that perpetuates the poverty of others. Yet, It is the Lord who helps them think decisively for the suffering of others. They feel within themselves to be kind and generous to the poor. These families are not wealthy families with much money. But they have a heart to feel for others. They are gracious to give and to know how the poor are helped. It is said that of all the countries, Americans are the most generous people in the world.

In the Old Testament, the poor were referred to as the Anawim of Yahweh. *Anawim* is the Hebrew word referring to those people who were economically poor, and socially suppressed. Prayers in the Book of Psalms testify to their desperate situation that drove them to take refuge in God: "In you, Lord, I take refuge; let me never be put to shame" (Ps 31:2). "Here I am, afflicted and poor. God, come quickly! You are my help and deliverer. Lord, do not delay" (Ps 70:6). "Hear me, LORD, and answer me, for I am poor and oppressed" (Ps 86:1). These prayers give us an idea about how the society looked down on the poor. The words *shame, afflicted, oppressed* take us to the social stigma attached to the poor in the society.

What made the poor take refuge in the Lord was their dependence on God's promise. Old Testament people had experienced protection from God, and so there emerged people's dependence on God. The poor would remind themselves of God's promise, and His acts of protection to them: You sent deliverance to your people, ratified your covenant for ever; holy and awesome is your name" (Ps 111:9). "All who call up on me I will answer: I will be with them in their distress; I will deliver them and give them honor" (Ps 91: 15). The poor had a reason to take refuge in God as they were motivated by the experience of the past. They knew God was present with them to take care of them. The way God took care of them was to motivate each one to care for others: "The needy will never be lacking in the land; that is why I command you to open your hand to your poor and needy kinsman in your country" (Dt 15:11).

The kingdom of God is the presence of God in Jesus that motivates one to give and care for the poor. Jesus proclaimed, "The Spirit of God is upon me, because he has anointed me to bring glad tidings to the poor" (Lk 4:18b). In Jesus, God is present to the poor. His Presence makes the rich take care of the poor. He advocated detachment from material possessions in the parable of the Rich Fool (Lk 12:16-21). This "detachment" is the generous and radical decision to part with one's possessions to be given to the poor and the needy.

St. Paul calls the act of generosity righteousness. Righteousness is the noble act of God. Those who give to the poor have the godlike behavior of righteousness. He blesses them. When you give to the poor "God will supply and increase the harvest of your righteousness" (2 Cor 9:10b). St. Basil the Great, who is a powerful advocate of the poor, expounds on St. Paul's idea of righteousness: "Your reward for the right use of the things of this world will be everlasting glory, a crown of righteousness, and the kingdom of heaven. God will welcome you; the angels will praise you; all men who have existed since the world began will call you blessed."[2]

The Eucharistic Presence of Jesus continues to make righteous people give to the poor. In dying for others, the act of righteousness became the meritorious example of love for the poor. As the Risen Lord, Jesus is present in the Eucharist to enable millions and millions of people to be generous to the poor. The loving presence of Jesus, in the words of St Augustine, can be inspiring to all of us: "What does love look like? It has the hands to help others. It has the feet to haste to the poor and needy. It has the eyes to see misery and want. It has the ears to hear the sighs and sorrows of men. That is what love looks like."[3]

My Personal Context:

I am blessed with God's own behavior of righteousness. It is not my own human decision to be concerned about the poor. Rather it is the divine Presence in me that motivates me to be conscious of the poor. When I act on behalf of the divine Presence, Jesus makes me a righteous person.

Meditation:

After the preparatory steps:

I have breathed into me the Presence of Jesus. His Presence in me makes me an instrument of righteousness. I am awakened all the time to the cries of the poor. Let me submit to

His Presence to be of help, support, and comfort to the poor. *Let me pray: Lord Jesus, Your Presence in me makes me feel for others. It makes me all the more conscious of the poor. Let me never ignore the sufferings of the poor. Let me do whatever I can to be righteous in your Presence, to be a blessing to the poor, so that I can join the Psalmist to thank the Lord in his words:*

> *Let them thank the Lord for such kindness,*
> *Such wondrous deeds for mere mortals*
> *For he satisfied the thirsty,*
> *Filled the hungry with good things (107:8,9).*

27. I Grow in Mercy for the Sinners

*Mercy is the ultimate expression of love
and is that which fulfills it.*
Chiara Lubich[1]

The late Fr. Joseph Harou, a French missionary, was a remarkable Spiritual Director at St Peter's Seminary, Bangalore, India. He said something very powerful during one spiritual conference: "As future priests to sit in the confessional, never assume yourself to be a judge; rather be like the Father who waits for the prodigal son." His practical glimpses of advice on this statement have guided so many of us in the confessionals. Accordingly, from my experience, I can state two of the pastoral outcomes of many confessions.

The first is about people who come for confessions after many long years. I make it a point to say a word of welcome to make them comfortable. Second, when people say that they don't remember the Act of Contrition, I tell them gently to pray with their own spontaneous act of contrition. One such Act of Contrition I paraphrase here: "Lord, I am not worthy to be counted among the ones who can receive your mercy; yet have me as a prodigal son. Help me not to sin any more." This prayer amazed me, as the prayer is biblical in its content.

Confession is a 'Prodigal Experience.' The word 'Prodigal' means "extravagant, spendthrift." This made the son prodigal. The Father too is an "extravagant, spendthrift" of His mercy on the return of the son. This makes him 'prodigal' too. And so confession is the Prodigal Experience of the extravagance of mercy and the extravagance of sin. The parables of the Lost Sheep, the Lost Coin, and the Lost Son are the most illustrative of the Prodigal Experience.

Why was Jesus so illustrative of God's mercy? Our understanding, in the context of this chapter, should take into account the very origin of *mitzvah* in the OT history. Mitzvah in Hebrew cannot find a parallel word in any other language. It is because Mitzvah is not just a word for commandment or law, as some would try to translate it. Mitzvah includes the 613 commandments of both positive directions (thou shall do) and negative restrictions (thou shall not do). It includes the daily obligation to fulfill them, and the rewards of righteousness. Above all, Mitzvah derives its force and authority from the Holy God: "For I, the Lord, am your God; and you shall make and keep yourselves holy, because I am holy" (Lv 11:44). God alone is Holy. Mitzvah is meant to make the observant holy, i.e. just and right; but the very act of observance is possible only by relying on God's righteousness. One cannot be righteous by his own merit. So Mitzvah is the result of *being close to God.*

In the course of the OT history, Mitzvah lost its very essence as the giver and the origin of righteousness was put aside.

Mitzvah became just the norms of laws for any one to strive to be righteous. Self-righteousness is the result of people who gradually lost sight of God's strength to be righteous. Instead it made them rely on their own vainglory. During the time of Jesus, self-righteousness was more evident. Another fact to keep in mind is that self-righteous people are likely to be judgmental so as to watch others to approve or to condemn. The behavior of so many Pharisees and Scribes was shocking to Jesus. They were self-righteous to condemn others.

The category of "sinners" included the tax collectors, known also as Publicans. They were employed by the Romans to collect taxes from the Jewish territories under them. There was plenty of room for extortion, so that after paying the Romans, they could also keep money for themselves and so they were considered traitors and cheats.

"Sinners" also included prostitutes. Prostitution in ancient culture was the consequential evil of pagan practice. They believed to have had a special relationship with gods or goddesses through prostitution. Another system that perpetuated that evil was the patriarchal system that regarded men as superior, to do whatever they wanted to with women. The people of Israel, gathered around one true God, knew that prostitution was never acceptable to God: "There shall be no temple harlot among the Israelite women, nor a temple prostitute among the Israelite men" (Dt

23:18). Yet, there were evidences of temple harlotry. Prophet Hosea warned them, "Because they have abandoned the LORD to practice harlotry" (Hos 4:10). Jeremiah reprimanded them, "You defiled the land by your wicked harlotry" (Jer 3: 2b).

"Sinners" also included the so-called "People of the Land". They were supposed to have been left out in the land during the time of the exile to Babylon. Eventually they happened to marry the Gentiles. One such *people of the land* were the Samaritans, who were rejected as outcasts on the ground of racial purity.

What made Jesus identify Himself with the sinners? First, Jesus was the One who would *understand* the situation that made them sinners. Sinners themselves don't know why they sin, and this is always the sad predicament of sinners. And St. Paul himself said it, "What I do I do not understand. For I do not do what I want, but I do what I hate" (Rom 7:15). On the part of people who judge them, as the simple reasoning goes: *where there is perfect understanding there is no condemnation.* Jesus understood their situation and so did not condemn them. This does not mean He justified the sins. His mercy would surpass the legality of condemnation. That is why Jesus was ready to forgive them (Lk 7:48).

Second, Jesus knew that the sinners relied on the mercy of God unlike the self-righteous. That is what motivated Jesus to tell them the parable of the Pharisee and the Publican (Lk 18:9-14). The Pharisee was not justified because he exposed his self-righteousness by comparing his 'righteous deeds' with the sins of the Publican. The Publican went home justified because he relied on God's mercy. "Justified" brings back the true experience of *being close to God,* which was the very purpose of Mitzvah. Jesus restored Mitzvah to its right place of *the closeness* of God. Jesus said, "I have not come to abolish the law but to fulfill it" (Mt 5:7). He wanted *to be close* to them. He would go out of the way to eat with sinners (Mk 2:15). This is the reason why Jesus was very forceful in saying: "I did not come to call the righteous but sinners" (Mk 2:17b).

The actual Mitzvah experience comes true in Jesus, present in the Eucharist. He *is close* to us to make us righteous. St. Paul says it all: "But when the kindness and generous love of God our savior appeared, not because of any righteous deeds we had done but because of his mercy...." (Tit 3: 5). In Jesus we have the closeness of the mercy of God.

My Personal Context:

My closeness to Jesus in the Eucharist helps me to recognize His mercy for me, a sinner. This in turn helps us to be merciful to others. Let me hear what St. Julian of Norwich has to say: "Looking on another person's sin, we cannot see the fair beauty of God, unless we look on these sins with contrition along with the sinner; with compassion for the sinner; and with a holy desire to God on behalf of the sinner."[2]

Mediation:

After the preparatory steps:

I am conscious of my closeness to Jesus. He is within me. His presence in me makes me just and right. The more I realize my righteousness the more I realize I am a sinner. Let me never be self-righteous. Let me pray; *Lord, You are merciful to me; let me be merciful to others. Let my life be always a witness to the closeness of Your Presence in me and to the mercy by which You guide me. Let this part of the Psalm echo in my heart:*

Restore my joy in your salvation;

Sustain in me a willing spirit.

I will teach the wicked your ways,

that sinners may return to you (51:14, 15).

28. I Grow in Love for Children

Every child comes with the message
that God is not yet discouraged of humanity.

Rabindranth Tagore[1]

.

Little Kaitlyn's parents invited me home for dinner. When I reached their home I rejoiced at the sign that was posted on the door. The sign read: **Welcome to our home, Fr. Dhas.** *It was a beautiful drawing by Kaitlyn. The child was so excited the whole day, according her parents, to draw the sign herself. It was one of the joyous moments of my life to witness something very interesting about a child's innocence. After dinner, I asked for that sign to take it along with me. It tells me that a child is so different from adults. In the normal parlance of adult life, the adults would be concerned about what others would say or think about the sign on the door. The child does not care one way or the other about what others think. Usually as adults, one's nationality, color, class, etc may govern our sentiments. Here is a child, who sees a priest as a priest. Nothing of my Indian nationality, color, or accent matters to the child.*

Another example is little Giovanni from the second grade. One Sunday coming out after Mass Giovanni said to me, "Fr. Dhas, I am your fan." I asked him, "Why do you want to be my fan?" He said smilingly, "I like the way you say Mass." There is no hypocrisy at all in this child to say something like that, which is beyond biased sentiments.

It is no wonder why Jesus brought in a child to point out the narrow-mindedness of the adults who took offense at Him because of His family, place, work etc (Mk 6:1-6).He brought the child as a model for others. His teaching about the child has twofold implications: one is *to receive* the child and the other is *to become* like a child. Receiving a child, in the mind of Jesus, entails an experience of mystical union with God. Jesus said, "Whoever receives one child as this in my name, receives me, and whoever receives me, receives not me but the One who sent me"(Mk 9:37). This is one of the many simple but emphatic sayings of Jesus about children becoming the means of the mystical connection with God. When a child is loved and cared for, one can have the mystical connection with God. As it is the case with any mystical experience, this too comes with some profound responsibilities.

First, such a child can never be ignored or neglected but rather *be received*. Jesus became indignant at his disciples when they tried to prevent the children from coming to Him. Jesus said, "Let the children come to me; do not prevent them" (Mk 10:14). This means that everyone should be responsibly aware of the presence of children, and they cannot neglect them as insignificant. Second, children can never be abused. Jesus teaches this as a grave responsibility to the extent of saying, "a great millstone hung around his neck and to be drowned in the depths of the sea" (Mt 18:6). Failing in this responsibility is seen as a cry against heaven: "… their angels in heaven always look upon the face of my heavenly Father" (Mt 18:10). This teaching binds every one in such a manner that all should take extraordinary care to be exemplary to the children.

'Becoming' is the other implication of the teaching of Jesus about children. Becoming a child calls for an inner experience. Becoming is creating in us the healthy ego that respects the inner presence of God. It is a subjective experience. Seeing a child objectively as a model is not enough. It should become a subjective experience for all. Jesus, the Son of God, Himself born a child, bore witness to the subjective experience. His birth became a model of humility; and so a child in its reality becomes a model for humility. Inviting others to become a child, He Himself 'became a child' in all He said and did.

Becoming surpasses the dictates of the ego to appreciate all the goodness in all. It surpasses the indifference of group mentality to appreciate others. Jesus did that when his disciples tried to stop others from doing good deeds. Jesus said, "Do not prevent them. There is no one who performs a mighty deed in my name who can at the same time speak ill of me"(Mk 9:39). *Becoming* attributes our own goodness to God, and not to one's own ego. Jesus himself becoming a child, said to Philip, "The Father who dwells in me is doing his work" (Jn 14:10b). *Becoming* surpasses the ego limitations of superior-inferior considerations. Jesus becoming a child says to his disciples, "if anyone wishes to be first, he shall be the last of all and the servant of all" (Mk 9:35*). Becoming* surpasses public recognition of titles and honors to serve all. Jesus becoming the child did that: "You call me a 'teacher' and 'master' rightly so, for indeed I am. If I therefore, the master and teacher, have washed your feet, you ought to wash one another's feet" (Jn 13:12). These and many other examples of Jesus inspired his own disciples to become children.

St. Paul manifests 'the becoming of a child' in his life and mission. All along his mission, he had that childlike conviction. He attributed his work to his Master, Jesus Himself: "I have the strength for everything through him who empowers me" (Phil 4: 13). Becoming like a child is to have no ego complex, as St. Paul would say, "I have made myself a slave to all so as to win over as many as possible" (1 Cor 9:19). St. Paul became a child to surpass narrow mindedness: "I have become all things to all, to save at least some" (1 Cor 9:23). The practical advice of Paul is appropriated at the end of the process of becoming a child: "Do nothing out of selfishness or out of vainglory; rather, humbly regard others as more important than yourselves, each looking out not for his own interests, but everyone for those of others" (Phil 2:3).

Jesus' examples of becoming a child in His life and mission truly manifest his inner truth; that is the experiencing of the Kingdom of God within Himself. That is why His compelling statement, "Amen I say to you, unless you turn and become like children, you will not enter the kingdom of heaven" (Mt 18:3). As we have already seen in the previous chapters, the Kingdom of heaven is the Presence of God in Jesus. The Presence of God in Jesus embraces every human being on earth. It is always a process, which has to begin with the recognition of God's presence with us in the world.

The Presence of God is in the Eucharist. It is in the Eucharist Jesus animates each one of us to become like a child. Jesus is mystically connected to every one beyond ones color, nationality, status or power. In His Presence we become humble to acknowledge His own image in everyone. We allow ourselves to become a child in our inner self, which manifests outwardly in our recognition of others' goodness. The inner self now begins to follow the ways of Jesus Himself becoming a child in all we say and do.

My Personal Context:

It is the presence of Jesus in the Eucharist that connects me; it is Jesus in the Eucharist, who connects me to everyone.

And so I am connected to all in Jesus. By accepting the invitation of Jesus to become like a child and the advice of St. Paul to seek always the interests of others, I will be one of the "little ones" (Mk 9:42) of Jesus. I shall be aware of the mystical connection that is always in force within me in receiving the Eucharist.

Meditation:

After the preparatory step:

I have breathed Jesus into me; I am aware of my connection with others in Jesus. May this mystical connection transform me to become a child, and to be counted among the little ones. May I remind myself of the eternal prayer, and make it my own to pray: *Lord Jesus, You experienced the mystical connection with your Father at the very thought of all the little ones. Help me to rejoice with you by becoming childlike. May I be one with you in thanking the Father for this mystical union in the words of the Psalmist:*

> *Out of mouths of babe and infants*
> *You have drawn a defense against your foes(8:3).*

29. I Grow in Respect for Women

One of the ways in which Jesus turned his world up-side down was by giving women exactly the same value and dignity as men.

Albert Nolan[1]

Dr. Antoinette Gutzler, MM is a Catholic feminist theologian, living and working in Taiwan. Dr. Antoinette, as a Woman Religious, is researching Asian Christology to educate and liberate Asian women who suffer from oppressive cultural traditions. I had a few occasions to meet her when she visited her sister Barbara who lives in our parish. One of her papers is titled, "Navigating the Tradition: A Christian Feminist Perspective on the Power of Creedal Language to Shape the Lives of Women." It has a graphic description of the situation of Asian women:

In Asia, Women are sold into sex-slave business through trafficking, they are raped as a "spoils" of war, and men desiring obedient and submissive wives "buy" their mail order brides from Southeast Asia. Oppression of women by women continues in the traditional opposition between mother-in-law and daughter-in-law in Chinese culture, dissatisfaction over dowry payments has led to the burning deaths of

181

young brides in India, while others, in oppressive marriages and family situations in Afghanistan, find a way out by burning themselves with kerosene...

Cultures have come a long way to liberate human civilization from oppressive traditions of inequality. Yet, in the light of what is achieved all over the world, we become critical about some cultures that are so stagnant as to preserve oppressive cultural traditions. Anyone with a right mind cannot tolerate or overlook the oppressive cultures. Education is the key. Sr. Gutzler, like many others, is prophetic to take up the task of education to bring about equality between men and women so as to preserve the respect and dignity of humanity. There have been many studies to educate men and women of their equality. Just to cite a recent study by UNICEF, it reports, "Inequality at home between man and woman leads to poorer health for the children and greater poverty of the family." It is again the oppressive cultures that pose this difficult situation.

Admittedly, culture is shaped to a large extent by one's own religion. Scholars such as historians and theologians constantly revisit religious traditions to eradicate oppressive structures that are perpetuated in the name of God. Christian theologians have been remarkable in studying the oppressive structures of culture in the light of the scriptures. In our own times, the late Pope John Paul II called it an urgent task to end unjust structures of inequality between men and women: "It is urgently necessary to cultivate everywhere a culture of equality, which will be lasting and constructive to the extent that it reflects God's plan" (Angelus, June 1995). Ultimately, eradication of oppressive structures is to realize God's plan, which wills to change the face of the world.

The Book of Genesis is the foundational source to understanding the equality between men and women. The date of writing the Book of Genesis, which is 1440-1400 BC, coincides with the dominance of Mesopotamian culture of a patriarchal society; this culture perpetuated the subjugation of women to men. One would expect that the sacred authors would succumb to the patriarchal influence; they were rather faithful to the truth, and not to the culture. Unfortunately, the patriarchal culture of our own times interpreted the Book of Genesis in an unfair way against women.

Thanks to the scholarship of fair minds, the unfair interpretation of the Book of Genesis is being clarified and rectified. A few verses of the creation story will fit into the context of this chapter. First, "God created **man** in His own image; in the divine image he created **him**; male and female he created them" (Gen 1: 27). One may read this as man was created first and so woman is second to him. Actually "Man" in Hebrew is *Adam.* The precise translation is humankind, and if we translate it as man, it is in a generic sense, and not in the gender sense. God created humanity simultaneously as man and woman. And so woman is not a secondary person.

Second, "It is not good for the man to be alone. I will make a **suitable partner** for him" (Gen 2:18). "Suitable partner" used to be translated as "helper." The word "helper" in Hebrew is "ezer," which does not imply *inferiority or subordination*. On the contrary, the word connotes the support of a superior person. But it is not about superiority or inferiority that is implied here, rather the *equality* of man and woman. And so *"suitable partner'* is close to the right translation.

Third, "The Lord God then built up into a woman **the rib** that he had taken form the man" (Gen 2:22). This is often taken as woman was created to be subordinate, to be a helper to man as she came from his rib. *"From his rib"* really means an essential partner, as woman is made from the same body. It refers to the equality of man and woman.

The creation story is about man and woman, complementary to each other with God's image imprinted in both of them as man and woman. In the words of Pope John Paul II, " In the unity of the two, man and woman are called from the beginning not only to exist 'side by side' or 'together', but that are also called to exist mutually one for the other"(#7 Apostolic letter, *Mulieris Dignitatem*).

Jesus, the Son of God, born of a woman bears witness to the dignity of gender and its functions. Jesus raised the issue of the equality of man and woman in the patriarchal dominance of his own times and culture. His miracles for women (Jn 11:1-44), and having women as disciples (Mk 15:41), are some of the examples of how Jesus counted on the equality of men and women. St. Paul took it from Jesus to say, "…there is not male and female; for you are all one in Christ Jesus" (Gal 3:28). The presence of Jesus in the Eucharist is an invitation to restore this equality. We, the men and women, share one cup and one body in the Eucharist. As Pope Benedict XVI exhorts us, Eucharist should continue "to transform unjust structures and to restore respect for the dignity of all men and women, created in God's image and likeness."[2]

My Personal Context:

In Jesus I have been brought to my awareness that the Church does not condone the unjust structures that subordinate women. In the Body of Christ, all men and women are one, and everyone is called to challenge any attitude that goes against the Body of Christ. I shall never give into the impact of some cultures that ill-treat women. May it be my way to tell them that women are not 'things', but persons imbued with the Image of God.

Meditation:

After the preparatory steps:

I am conscious of my image that is in equality with all my brothers and sisters. By respecting every woman, I respect my own body that is one with the Body of Jesus. Let the awareness grow in me as I begin to pray: *Jesus, My Lord, let me uproot my own inner and outer expressions of abusive motives. Let me be the instrument of love and respect for all men and women to sing of human dignity along with the Psalmist:*

> *You have made them (us) little less than a god,*
> *Crowned them with glory and honor (8: 6).*

Notes:
Chapter 23
1.   Elizabeth A Dreyer, *Earth Crammed with Heaven* (NY/Mahwah: Paulist Press, 1994) p.78.
2.   www. the real presence.org, Quotes on the Most Blessed Sacrament.#3
Chapter 24
1.John C.Haughey,S.J, *Alternative futures for worship,Vol 3*,ed.Bernard J. Lee(Minnessota:The liturgical Press, 1987), p. 63.
3.   Pope Benedict XVI, *Jesus of Nazareth*, (NY: Doubleday Publication, 2007), p. 57.
Chapter 25
1. Genevieve Glen, OSB, *Introduction, The catholic Handbook for visiting the sick and the homebound,* (Chicago: LTP, 2008), p.1.
Chapter 26
1. Cummings Owen, *Eucharistic Doctors*, (New York/ Mahwah: Paulist Press, 2005), p.24.
2. Quote from *The liturgy of Hours,* (NY: Catholic Book publishing Co, Vol 3) p. 552.
3. www. Thinkexist.com- Quote from St Augustine. For the poor.
Chapter 27
1. Chiara Lubich, *Living City* (magazine) Oct 2009 Vol 48. #10-article: A spirituality of reconciliation.p.9.
2. Ritamary Bradley, *Praying with Julian of Norwich*, (Mystic, CT: Twenty Third Publications, 1995), p.150.
Chapter 28
1. www.brianyquote.com/rabindranath_tagore
Chapter 29
1.Albert Nolan, *Jesus today,* (NY: Orbis books, Maryknoll, 2006), p. 52.
2.Pope Benedict XVI, *The Sacrament of Charity,*(USSCB publication#7,2007),p.75.

VI. My Integrity

30. I Integrate the 'Anima' Within Me

Each of us contains within ourselves an
image of the opposite sex, which vitally
effects how we deal with other people.

James Arraj[1]

Tillie and Vincent are married 53 years. They are a very happy couple and always have a smile that is indicative of their love for each other. Whenever I see them in the church, I tell them, "Here comes the smiling couple." They smile all the more. One time I asked Tillie, "Tell me what is the secret behind your smile?" She said, "I can say the Lord is good to us. We are a happy couple." I proceeded to ask Tillie, "Then tell me what is the secret of the success of your marriage?" She said, "I should tell you I am blessed with Vincent. There is something about him that he is always there for me; he is always there for others. He thinks of others firsts."

Another couple, John and Carol, who celebrated their 50th wedding anniversary, wanted me to come to their home to renew their vows. Carol is bed ridden for a number of years with oxygen attached. John stood close to her bed and held her hand to renew their marriage vows. When it was time to say, 'in sickness in health,' they were moved to tears, and along with them their *sons and daughters. At the end of the ceremony, Carol said, "John is the best thing that has ever happened to my life."*

Vincent and John are the examples of men who, according to the theory of Carl Jung, have integrated their Anima within them.

While there are many theories to understand men and their behavior, let us choose to go with Carl Jung's *animus and anima*. Without going into the details of animus and anima, we shall only highlight what is necessary in the context of the chapter.

Animus is the masculine component in a woman. It is influenced by the genes of her father, and early childhood rapport with her brothers, uncles and other men. Anima is the feminine component in a man. It is influenced by his mother's genes and the relationship with his sisters, aunts and other women in his childhood development. In a society where the gender ideals have been defined for men to have assertiveness, achievement, competitiveness, dominance etc., and women to have animation, compliance, passivity, tenderness etc., animus and anima are keys to understanding our behavior towards the opposite sex.

Animus and anima are of the unconscious realm; men and women are not conscious of them. Yet these unconscious components are at the heart of every interaction between men and women. It is because *anima* is the feminine quality of a man, and *animus* is the masculine quality of a woman. The self has both conscious and unconscious sides. The unconscious side has to animate the conscious self to become whole. Anima of the unconscious side of a man has to be integrated to become the wholeness of his self.

When a man consciously integrates his anima with his self, his masculinity is seen in four operative styles: *mother, companion, solitary and visionary.*[2] Mothering is the genuineness to give. Companioning is about intimacy of giving and receiving. Solitary is about the independence to be courageous. Visionary is to plan for future security. When a wife experiences these anima-qualities in her husband, he becomes the man of her heart.

Integration helps the growth and wholeness of their relation as husband and wife. Man's failure to integrate anima creates *moods* in him. Woman's failure to integrate animus creates *opinions* in her. 'Moods' and 'opinions' are behind all the troubles between husbands and wives. As simplistic as this may look, it creates an awareness of what men and women need to do to grow in wholeness.

Integrating animus or anima is a process of transformation, which entails a conscious way of becoming. As Philip St. Romain put it, "Every person is a Self-becoming. If you know this for yourself, you will see it in others."[3] Man is said to be self-becoming when he himself is able to see how he manifests his strength, which was never there from the beginning. It is the same way with a woman. When both man and woman become 'self-becoming,' they are transformed into a whole; they are able to surmount any sort of moods and opinions, to be for each other. The 'self giving' will now care, appreciate, and encourage one another unconditionally. His/Her self-becoming is a key to become self-giving to others.

When we look at Jesus, we see the perfect integration of his anima with the self. The integration is holistic that Jesus went to the extent of saying, "My Father and I are one" (Jn 10:30). Applying Jungian concepts to Jesus, His *mothering* is experienced by all. When men, women, children flocked to Him as He said, "Come to me, all you who labor and are burdened and I will give you rest" (Mt 11:28). His *companioning* is experienced by John, James and Peter, who were present with Jesus at all important occasions like the transfiguration (Mt 17:1), and the agony in the garden (Mt 26:37). His *solitary* ways to be courageous is seen in the way he wanted to lay down his life: "I lay it down on my own" (Jn 10.18). His *visionary* future is magnificently manifested in His Presence in the Eucharist and eternal life. Jesus said, "Do not work for food that perishes but for the food that endures for eternal life, which the Son of Man will give" (Jn 6: 27). All these and many other qualities testify to the fact of Jesus' self-giving to others.

The finale of the Self-giving of Jesus is the institution of the Eucharist. It is the complete Self-giving of Jesus to humanity. As Anthony F. Campbell says, "Christ's Body and Blood, the laying down of his own life for love of human life and for his friends, reveals to us the depths of God's love and so brings salvation to the whole world."[4] Every person's self-becoming thus can draw the same energy from the Eucharist.

My Personal Context:

The more I am conscious of my masculinity, the more I become aware of my anima-potential to be integrated within me. Self-becoming is not the result of one time conscious move to integrate my anima. It is a process, and it is possible only with the gift of Eucharist. My Self has to become one with Jesus. It has to become more of Christ's self, and less of myself. Christ's self-giving will enable me to integrate the anima within me. As Teilhard De Chardin would pray: "It was a joy to me O God, in the midst of the struggle, to feel that in developing my self I was increasing the hold that you have upon me." [5]

Meditation:

After the preparatory steps:

I am conscious of my body.....I am conscious of my masculinity.... I am conscious of the unconscious side of my self. Now that Christ has become one within me, let my self begin to integrate my anima.....Let me pray: *O Lord Jesus, Your self-*

becoming is the self-giving to me and to others. Let me keep in mind others in my life as I begin to integrate my anima. Let my self become a self-giving person like You. Let me be assured of Your continuous hold on me as I shall join the Psalmist:

> *My help comes from the Lord*
> *the maker of heaven and earth(121:2).*

31. I Integrate My 'Animus' Within Me

A woman's masculine qualities can be a very positive part of her personality, and so can a man's feminine qualities. The one acts like "spirit" and the other like "soul," enlivening life and opening up new horizons.

John A. Sanford[1]

George and Joan are married for 50 years. When they come to church on Sundays, they sit in the very first pew in order to give undivided attention to the Eucharistic celebration. They are very attentive to the homilies, and as they come out of the Church they thank the priests for the homily. One Sunday George was telling me about his health problem, and the surgery he had to go through, and Joan was so concerned about him that she was emotional to ask for prayers. As I said a few words of encouragement to console Joan, George said about Joan, "Joan has tremendous faith in prayer. I don't know what I would do without her." Here is a genuine couple who can strengthen each other with their values in their life.

Joan is one of thousands and thousands of women, who have integrated the animus in them. They may not be the conscious of "animus"- integration per se as the psychologists suggest. Yet it could be the result of the unknown ways of integrating "animus" within them.

*Now that we have explored the theory of C. Jung to understand the "anima" integration within a man, we shall proceed to know the power of animus integration within a woman. Among many traits of animus, psychologists would include four traits: **Eternal Youth, Hero, Father, and Sage.***

Eternal Youth is the gentle but engaging nature to win others for a noble cause or mission; such a person becomes an organizer. *Hero* is the formidable character to be courageous to act for something right and just; such a person will stand by others to be assertive. *Father* is the empowering style to encourage others with knowledge and power; such a person stands out as a spiritual mentor. *Sage* is the one who is able to see God within his own self; such a person becomes self-disciplined to be a comforter and a guru for others.

It may be helpful to distinguish between partial and perfect integration of these traits. It may not be possible for every woman to integrate all four traits with equal force. When faced with a person, situation, or relationship one may integrate more of one trait than the other; depending on the need one may even have all four traits to a partial degree.

Perfect integration of all the four traits brings out women like Blessed Mother Theresa, and Dorothy Day to accomplish extraordinary missions. In the context of every woman and especially in the context of married life, partial integrity of these traits would make a harmonized pact with those of the husband, as is the case with Joan and George.

Mary, the mother of Jesus and other New Testament women are examples of *animus-integrated* persons. Mary setting out to travel to the hill country is on an engaging journey. She is able to go all the way to visit Elizabeth to become enthusiastic about the coming of the Messiah (Lk 1:39). Mary and other women were able to have their *hero* character in following Jesus in His way of the cross and standing by the cross: "Standing by the cross of Jesus were his mother, and his mothers sister, Mary the wife of Clopas, and Mary of Magdala" (Jn 19:25). The Apostles experienced Mary's empowering style of a Father after the Resurrection of Jesus: "All these devoted themselves with one accord to prayer, together with some women, and Mary the mother of Jesus and his brothers" (Acts 1:14). Luke describes Mary's sage style, when he says, "his mother kept all these things in her heart" (Lk 2:51b).

Mary's "animus" harmony was such that her life and mission were always seen in unison with Jesus her Son's life & mission. It is very interesting to note that there are saints like Augustine, Peter Damian, Bernard, Bonaventure, Albert the Great who have experienced the 'feminine' presence of Mary/ 'masculine' Presence of Jesus in the Eucharist.

For example, St. Augustine says, "We know, too, that in the Eucharist, together with the divinity, are the entire Body and Blood of Jesus taken from the body and blood of the Blessed Virgin. Therefore, at every Holy Communion we receive, it would be quite correct, and a very beautiful thing to take notice of our holy mother's sweet and mysterious presence, inseparably and totally united with Jesus in the Host. Jesus is ever her adored Son. He is the Flesh of her flesh and Blood of her blood."[2]

These great saints' experience of the Eucharist helps us experience the anima/animus integration within ourselves. When we are conscious of such integration, we can even have such a mystical experience. St.Therese of Lisieux would go to the extent of espousing Jesus in the Eucharist. Theresa calls Jesus in the Tabernacle, "Beloved Spouse," and "My Fiancée." Therese writes, " He, the king of kings, humbled Himself in such a way that His face was hidden, and no one recognized Him…and I, too, want to hide my face, I want my Beloved alone to see it."[3] This experience of Therese is neither sexual fantasy nor erotic compensation. It is the mystical way of integrating 'animus-experience' of Jesus' Presence in the Eucharist. The Eucharistic Presence of Jesus in as much as the real presence of Jesus can truly animate the animus experience.

My Personal Context:

Eucharist is the real presence of Jesus. I have the assurance of Jesus Himself: "For my flesh is true food, and my blood is true drink. Whoever eats my flesh and drinks my blood remains in me and I in him" (Jn 6:55, 56). Jesus comes into me and so He is in me. Receiving Jesus into me, as a woman I can experience His animus (as a man I can experience Mary's anima). Let me make a conscious effort to integrate *the animus-qualities of Jesus/anima qualities of Mary.* Just like Mary who had integrated her *animus* within her, now I shall integrate Jesus within me to strengthen my animus.

Meditation:

After the preparatory steps:

I am now conscious of Jesus present for my sake. I have received Him into me. He is the Animus of God who has come into me. Let me now be conscious of integrating all the beautiful traits of animus, for which I pray: *Lord Jesus I have the grace to acknowledge that you are the most perfect Animus of God. Having come into me, help me integrate your engaging nature; let me be courageous; let me be an empowering person; let me go beyond myself to be for others. I shall yearn for you Lord along with the Psalmist:*

My soul yearns and pines
for the courts of the lord.
My heart and flesh cry out
for the living God (84:2,3).

32. I Am Blessed by God!

We find ourselves to be most truly human
when we are raised to the level of the divine.

Thomas Merton[1]

Jeffrey is a sixth grader now. I can recall from his third grade, Jeffrey coming out of the church would greet the priests this way: " God bless you, Father!" He is serious in greeting this way. If I happen to be the first to say, "Jeffry God bless you," he would respond immediately, "God bless you too!" It is truly a human gesture on the part of Jeffrey, yet it is about imparting God's blessings.

In the confessionals, priests are accustomed to bless the people at the end of the confession. I am accustomed to say, "Go in peace and God bless you." Some would always respond, God bless you, too!" Though it is a spontaneous gesture, it is truly a human gesture on the part of the penitents to have been raised to the level of the divine. As a priest of God, I am ordained to bless the people by saying, "God bless you." But the human response to such a blessing is what raises the people to the divine. When we receive the blessing, the normal gesture is to say, "Thank you." But blessing the priest who blessed you is reflective of the very origin and the purpose of blessing.

The blessings we exchange with each other began with the story of creation. The creation account of Genesis reports three times of God's blessings: first to the creatures, second to the first parents, and the third on the seventh day. First, God *blessed* the creatures to be fertile, multiply, fill the water and the earth (Gen 1:22). By this blessing the creatures received the creative power. Second, after creating Adam and Eve God *blessed them* to be fertile, multiply, fill the earth and subdue it (Gen 1: 28). This *blessing* to Adam and Eve in Genesis was not to impart a *creative power* to them. It was more than that of a creative nature. It was an assurance of His Presence to them. Compared to the creatures, man alone can realize His Presence with them. God Himself would enunciate that assurance. For example, to Isaac: "I will *be with you*, and *bless you*" (Gen 26:3), to Jacob: "Know that I am with you" Gen 28:15). The third blessing on the seventh day is to celebrate the day for praising God for His assurance of His Presence.

As the Book of Genesis (6:11) reports, "In the eyes of God the earth was corrupt and full of lawlessness" except Noah who "walked with God" (Gen 6:10). In other words the lawlessness is about sin, and sin is ultimately about disregarding God's assurance of His "walking" presence. The flood destroyed all life on earth except Noah. God *blessed* Noah (Gen 9:1). This time it is to establish the covenant: "I am now establishing my covenant with you and your descendants after you" (Gen 9:9). Thus begins God's initiative to establish the New Covenant of Eucharist. It would be an assurance of His Presence in and through Jesus for humanity. And it would be the beginning of the celebration of humans blessing God.

"Blessing" is the translation of *Brakha*, which means to bestow the quality of the source. God as the source of giving is the giver. He gives his quality of His Presence as blessing. This Hebrew word, *Brakha* is closely connected to another word *Berekh* that means, "Knee." The one who receives the blessing receives it with profound respect to the giver. When God blessed the people, they responded in kneeling before Him to thank Him and to praise Him. It seems like an act of mutual blessing: on the part of God, *it is an assurance of His Presence for them*; on the part of people *it is to thank God for His Presence*. It is not that people blessed God; rather it was the way people acknowledged how blessed God is to bless them with His Presence.

One of the earliest references of such a blessing is in the words of Melchizedek, King of Salem. He brought out bread and wine, and being a priest of God most High, he blessed Abram with these words: *"Blessed be Abram by God Most high, the creator of heaven and earth; And blessed be God most high who delivered your foes into your hand"* (Gen 14:18-20). Melchizedek recognizing the blessings of God for Abram blessed

God for Abram. OT people recalled the blessings of God in their prayers by the opening words: "Blessed are you, Lord our God, King of the universe." It is interesting to note two of such ancient blessings are for bread and wine, which were the prayers before the meal known as *Qiddush:*

"Blessed are you, O lord God, king of the universe, who make bread come forth from the earth." "Blessed are you O lord God, king of the universe, who create the fruit of the vine."[2] These ancient prayers would become part of Eucharistic celebration. The institution of Eucharist is the reassurance of God's presence in the world, for which the people of God would come around to bless Him. *Eucharistia*, the Greek word, means *thanksgiving* for God's Presence in the world. As the Liturgical History professor Enrico Mazza puts it, "The thanksgiving commemorates and tells of God's gift; God is praised and his gift is praised in a single interior movement, since the gift is the revelation and manifestation of the giver."[3] Jesus is the revelation and manifestation of God.

Jesus "*said the blessing*" (Mt 14:22) is the continuation of God's act of blessing. Jesus' own presence is an act of blessing from God. How do we understand Jesus' blessing? St. Ambrose has a simple but profound insight into the blessing: "*Before the blessing with the heavenly words, the Eucharistic bread is called by another name; after the consecration it is called the body. He himself says that this is his blood. Before the consecration it is called something else. After the consecration it is called blood."*[4] this blessing makes us receive the body and blood so that we can experience His abiding presence.

In the OT God blessed the people to walk with Him. In the NT Jesus blessed the Bread and Wine, which becomes the Eucharist to abide within the receiver. In the OT, people were aware of God's presence with them, but not to the extent of our own awareness of *His abiding presence.* In the Eucharist we have God's abiding presence in us. The early Christians thanked God : *"We thank you, God Father of Jesus our Savior, for your holy name, which you have made to dwell in us, and for the knowledge, faith, charity and immortality which you have given us through Jesus your Servant."*[5] Thus we bless God for His own Son Jesus' presence with us and within us. When we bless God in the Presence of the Eucharist it becomes the greatest act of blessing.

My Personal Context:

Jesus has blessed me by His abiding presence in me. I cannot afford to ignore His presence in me. I shall ever honor and praise Jesus for His assurance of his abiding presence: "Whoever eats my flesh and drinks my blood remains in me and I in him" (Jn 6:56). I am the blessed as Jesus assured my blessedness: "Blessed are your eyes, because they see, and your ears, because they hear" (Mt 13:16). Recognizing His abiding presence has made me blessed. I have become all the more human to bless Him.

Meditation:

After the preparatory steps:

God's blessing has made me blessed to receive the Eucharist. My ears are blessed because I can hear Jesus' blessings for me in the Eucharist. Jesus blesses me and I bless him in adoration. My eyes are blessed because I see Jesus with me. Let me thank Jesus: *Lord Jesus I adore you for your presence within me. I thank you for you for making me more human in all I say and do with your presence within me. Let me join the Psalmist to sing your presence*

> *Every day I will bless you;*
> *I will praise your name for ever (145:2).*

33. I See the Blessedness of People and Places

Blessed are those who do not take life for granted,
for they are within measurable distance of taking it
as granted by God.

Ronald Rolheiser[1]

Stephanie, a college student, her brother Jonathan, a senior in High School, and Noelle, the youngest in middle school are great kids. All of them come to church along with their parents. People who see them have something nice to say about them. One person said to me, "Those kids are so reverential at the altar." Another time someone else exclaimed, "There is something great about these kids." These affirmations from the parish community led me to talk with Stephanie and Jonathan.

I mentioned to them those affirmative statements of the people about their love and respect to God and others. They were humble to admit that they are not perfect. Yet they agreed that they inherited these as parental blessings. About their reverential participation at the altar as servers, I asked them, "Where did you get the goodness to be so respectful and reverential in the church?" Stephanie, said, "Though my parents taught me as a child, now it is my turn to grow in that understanding. I think that is what makes me to be reverential in the church." Jonathan's reply was something similar to that of his sister, but a different approach. He said, "As a child, yes, my parents guided me. The time has come that I should be responsible to decide for myself. I enjoy coming to mass and being part of it with respect and reverence. I love it." This is what the parental blessings can do to their children. They grow in respect to places and persons.

Blessings are from God to the parents, and they in turn become a blessing to the children. The Book of Genesis helps us grasp this direction of God's blessings: "I will make your name great, so that you will be a blessing" (Gen 12:2). Such an assurance of blessing made Abram and his sons bless others. For example, Isaac blessed his son Jacob (Gen 28:1). All the blessings that took place in the OT are the sign of God's Presence that makes us bless others. Thus we see the beginning of what would become of Jesus' Presence in the Eucharist that would make places and persons sacred.

All the blessings of God in the OT were pointing towards Jesus, the Blessed one of God. The birth of Jesus was the highest form of recognition of the blessedness. That is why Elizabeth greeted Mary with such recognition of the blessedness: "Most Blessed are you among woman, and blessed is the fruit of your womb" (Lk 1:42). When the parents of Jesus brought him to be presented at the temple, Simeon blessed them (Lk 2: 34). Thus we see Jesus is the blessing, and in Him and for Him we can bless each other.

Let us look at Jesus' public ministry. All who came in touch with Him were blessed. Those who saw Him were considered blessed. All who heard Him were considered blessed. Jesus himself recognized the blessedness of people who would accept him, by seeing him and hearing him: "But blessed are your eyes, because they see and your ears because they hear" (Mt 13:16). It is the blessedness of Jesus that made the people to be poor in spirit, meek, peace seeking, merciful etc. The beatitudes are primarily about Jesus attributing his blessedness to all those who would live their values.

What we know of beatitudes are from Matthew and Luke. But each of them looked at Jesus from a different perspective of blessedness. Matthew saw Jesus as the mountain of blessing. So he placed the beatitudes as taught from the mountain. In the OT "Mountain" had a special significance in the life of the people. Mountain is the sign of God's presence. People would look up to the mountain for God's blessing (cf. Ps 121:1, Ps 24, 3). Luke saw Jesus' presence in our own place of living was becoming the blessing. And so Luke placed the beatitudes on the plain to tell us that God's Presence has come down to bless us in our own living place. For Luke, Jesus is not just like any other prophet who needs to go to the mountain to have God's blessing. Jesus Himself is the blessing as He is in our living place.

We can combine the two testimonials of Matthew and Luke to make a profound truth about Jesus' presence: "God of Mountains" (1Kg 11:29) has come down to be one with us in the plain. St. John makes this truth all the more dynamic: "And the Word became flesh and made his dwelling among us, and we saw his glory, the glory as of the Father's only son, full of grace and truth" (Jn 1:14). The Glory of God that was seen and experienced on the mountain (Ex 24:16) is now seen and experienced by us in Jesus. "Glory" is always associated with the blessings of His presence for us. And so, we can see God's glory in our place of living and have His blessings here on earth. St. Paul was unique in blessing God for such a blessing: "Blessed be God and Father of our Lord Jesus Christ who has blessed us in Christ with every spiritual blessing in the heavens" (Eph 1:3). *Every spiritual blessing in heaven* is right here with us in our own place of living.

Eucharist is His Presence. We don't have to go up to the mountains to have God's experience. Our place is made sacred and so it is incumbent on us to see all the places as sacred and all the people are to be respected. Take away the Eucharist, and no place is sacred; no one needs to be respected. Basically it is the Presence of God in the Eucharist that makes us respect place and persons.

My Personal Context:

Jesus has blessed me. Wherever I go the blessedness in me makes those places blessed. Whosoever I meet is blessed. All is seen blessed because all is seen in relation to Christ's Presence in me; nothing can be seen in isolation from Jesus. I need to heed what St. Paul tells me, "…all belong to you, and you to Christ, and Christ to God" (1Cor 3:22). In and through me, God is connected to my place and to others. As the Letter to the Hebrews says, "He who consecrates and those who are consecrated all have one origin" (Heb 2:11). It is in Christ each of us was consecrated from the foundation of the world.

Meditation:

After the preparatory steps:

Jesus has made his dwelling place in me; I am His tabernacle. Eucharist is connecting me to the blessedness of God, place and others. I become conscious of the place I live in, the persons I meet today. Let me pray: *O Lord Jesus, How fortunate I am when I realize the blessing of Your Presence in me. Your Presence makes me blessed. Make me today and all the days of my life to make my life blessed to consecrate all the places and all the persons I meet. Let me be conscious of the origin of my blessings to imprint it in my heart and mind:*

Bless the Lord, all creatures,

Everywhere in God's domain,

Bless the Lord, my soul! (103: 22).

Notes:

Chapter 30

1. James Arraj, *St.John of the cross and Dr.C.G.Jung* (Chiloquin, OR: Inner Growth Books, 1988)p.13.

2.Janice Brewi& Ann Brennan, *mid – life spirituality and Jungian Archetypes*, (York Beach, Maine: Nichas- Hays, 1999), p. 46.

3. St Philip St. Romain, *Caring for the self caring for the soul*, (Missouri: Ligouri/Triumph, 2000), Page12.

4. Teilhard de Chardin, *Divine milieu*, (NY: Harper Collins, 2001, p.56.

Chapter 31

1. John Sanford, *Between People*, (NY/Ramsay, NJ: Paulist Press, 1998), p.40.

2. St. Augustine's quote from www.the real presence .org

3. St Therese' quote from www.the realpresence.org

Chapter 32

1. Thomas Merton, *New man*, (NY: Farrar, Straus&Giroux, 1961, p.126.

2. EnrcoMazza, The *celebration of the Eucharist*, (Collegeville, Minnesota: Liturgical press, 1999), p.307.

3. Ibid., p.283.

4. Ibid., p. 68.

5. Ibid., p.309.

Chapter 33

1. Ronald Rolheiser, *The Shattered Lantern*, (NY: The Crossword Publishing Co., 2004), p.185.

VII. My Ministry

34. I Grow Outraged by the suffering of the Handicapped

> If we are going to be honest and sincere, as Jesus was, we must face the full horror of human suffering and allow ourselves to be outraged by the unimaginable cruelty of so many of our fellow human beings.
>
> Albert Nolan[1]

Timmy is one of the volunteers of the First Saturday Club that care for the handicapped. He has been involved for the past 33 years in this club. In 1971, this club emerged out of the inspiration of the then Pastor of St. Peter's Church, Hyde Park, Rev. Daniel O'Hare, who asked some of his parishioners to pick up the disabled for Sunday mass. After his transfer from the parish, Elizabeth DiStesano coordinated this ministry to bring 50 to 60 handicapped men and women together to pray the rosary on the First Saturday. Gradually they were in touch with the pastors of Dutchess County, NY, to have the Eucharistic celebration on First Saturday. Some parishes were generous to provide them with a lunch after the rosary and the mass.

It was at the age of 19, Timmy was moved by the suffering of one Victor who was not able to walk. He took him to the gathering on First Saturday for almost two and a half years. Then he helped Donald, who had lost his sight. Timmy and his wife Rita took care of Donald and when Donald passed away, they went to the extent of taking care of his funeral expenses. Now Timmy takes his own mother Barbara in a wheel chair to the gathering. Timmy's motivation to do this ministry: "This is the ministry where you can give without expecting anything in return; not even the sincere word of thanks." According to Timmy, there are two ways people say thanks: standard thanks of formality and the sincere thanks of the heart. "I could always notice the sincere thanks in their face! I am reluctant to accept even the sincere thanks. My entire family has a great fulfillment to see them happy at these gatherings. That is all that matters to us."

The people in the OT had terrible attitudes about the handicapped. They thought God was inflicting punishment on the children for their parents' wickedness. It was almost accepted as a curse inflicted by God as a punishment. One of such punishments was children born blind, lame etc. This attitude is one of those crude anthropomorphisms, i.e. human beings ascribing human ways to God, and upholding it as God's ways of dealing with humans. It is a necessary language pattern for the human mind without which humans cannot comprehend God's ways and to relate to others. Yet the same language pattern cannot afford to contradict the divine perfection. If that happens, then it is crude. One such crude anthropomorphism can be read from the Book of Exodus: "For I, the Lord, Your God am a jealous God, inflicting punishment for their fathers wickedness on the children of those who hate me, down to the third and fourth generations" (20:5). God who is All-Perfect cannot be "jealous" because it is a limitation. Also "inflicting punishment" on children is cruel.

This crude anthropomorphism was not acceptable to the minds of Jesus' disciples. They asked Jesus, "Rabbi, who sinned, this man or his parents, that he was born blind?" Jesus answered, "Neither he nor his parents sinned" (Jn 9:2,3). Jesus corrected the inhuman attitude that originated from the OT anthropomorphism. People even took offense at the healing of Jesus, as it was taken as Jesus going against God's way of punishment. Jesus asked them to change their attitude and to accept His mission of healing. It is evidenced in His reply to the messengers of John the Baptist: "Go and tell John what you hear and see: the blind regain their sight, the lame walk, lepers are cleansed, the deaf hear, the dead are raised, and the poor have the good news proclaimed to them. And blessed is the one who takes no offense at me" (Mt 11:4).

Jesus Himself was outraged by the apathy of the people towards the handicapped. He was angry and grieved at the hardness of their hearts (Mk 3:5). Being 'outraged' should not be taken as an emotional vent or set back. It is a breakthrough from the old ways of looking at things, and to act courageously on behalf of the handicapped. Jesus made the breakthrough that was continued after His resurrection by the mission of His own Apostles. Jesus' presence in Peter and John empowered them to cure the crippled man (Acts 3:6). It is very interesting to note what Peter and John said to the crippled man. Peter said to him, "I have neither silver nor gold, but what I do have I give you: in the name of Jesus Christ the Nazorean, rise and walk." What did they *have* that they *gave*? It was the Presence of Jesus in them they gave to the crippled man. It echoes the OT teaching of the Book of Deuteronomy.

In the OT, God made his *name* dwell in a place: "then to the place which the Lord, your God, chooses as the dwelling place for his name..." (Deut 12:11). Here the *name* means *God's Presence*. After the resurrection, the Apostles experienced the *name-Jesus* was dwelling in them. By the saying "what I do have" Peter meant the presence of the Name, Jesus. He said, "in the name of Jesus Christ, rise and walk." This way of experiencing the name of Jesus in them was very much the power of the early Church. Didache, one of the early Christian writings, testifies to this: "We thank you, Holy Father, for your Holy Name which you have caused to tabernacle in our hearts, and for the knowledge and faith, and immortality which you made known to us through Jesus your servant" (Chapter 10:2).[2] It was an awesome experience for the early church to have realized that

Jesus was in them; and so, in His Name they could have compassion for the handicapped. In their charitable deeds, the Name Jesus was in them to accomplish all for them.

The Name of Jesus Christ remains in us. Jesus has caused us to be the tabernacle for His Name to be present. Jesus' Presence in the Eucharist helps us to be outraged at the suffering of the people, rather than succumbing to be indifferent. His Presence makes it possible for humans to be sensitive to the suffering of the people. Ronald Rolheiser has rendered a healthy insight into the way that we can look at the handicapped: "Ask any family that has a handicapped member.... What they think has given them depth, compassion, and understanding...They will tell you.... It is weakness, limit, shame and powerlessness that bring depth."[3] Anyone who knows the struggles of the disabled would tell us about the true compassion and help. They have the compassionate heart of Jesus.

My Personal Context:

I am the tabernacle for His Name to dwell in me. With my sincerity and honesty, I am outraged like Jesus to see the suffering of others. As I experience the outrage, Jesus in me is reaching out to the suffering of the handicapped. I would admit the deep concern of anyone who lives with the handicapped. I should get to know their power and compassion. Let me be compassionate to them at all cost.

221

Meditation:

After the preparatory steps:

I am conscious of Jesus dwelling within me. I am going to be in touch with the suffering of the handicapped. Let my mystical connection be with him (her) as Jesus is reaching out to him (her). With my compassion let me pray: *Lord Jesus, I thank you for reaching out to my brother (sister) who is in need of your compassion. Let me bring them your constant love care and support. Let me join the Psalmist to resound his words within me, because God*

> *Heals the broken hearted,*
> *Binds up their wounds,*
> *Numbers all the stars*
> *Calls each of them by name (146:3,4).*

35. I Experience the Healing Touch of Jesus

> We know that touching adds a whole new
> dimension to verbal communication. We
> are "bodily" human beings, a close
> composite of body and soul, which work
> together in close cooperation. We should
> think of our senses as gifts of God and
> antennas of learning.
>
> John Powell[1]

Kristen, as a high school student, took up the Prayer Shawl ministry for the Girl Scout Gold Award from Girl Scouts Heart of the Hudson. It was in the fall of 2008, she was inspired by this creative ministry, which was innovated by Janet Bristow and Victoria Galo, two graduates of the 1997 Women's Leadership Institute at the Hartford Seminary, Hartford. The vision of the ministry is the care and love of knitting that is combined into a prayerful ministry that reaches out to those in need of comfort and solace. Many blessing are knitted into every shawl. They wrap, enfold, comfort, cover, give, mother, hug, shelter and beautify. In short, it is the healing touch of Jesus. Kristen has received many testimonials. I shall mention one from Georgina and Jack:

"Thank you so much for the lovely prayer shawl to Jack. Your thoughtful gift brought a smile to Jack's face. He has been wrapped in the shawl every chance he gets. It does help."

What Kristen started this as a Girl Scout Project became the ministry of her parents, Bill and Debbie. Now it has become one of the powerful healing ministries, and has been taken up by the Catholic Daughters –Court Queen of Peace #1534.As many as 40 shawls have been received by persons who needed the healing touch of Jesus.

The Incarnation of God in Jesus is the powerful manifestation of God's touch to the people. People realized this and so they brought the sick so that they could touch Jesus to be healed of their infirmities. Luke says, "Everyone in the crowd sought *to touch* him because *power came forth from him and healed them all"* (Lk 6:19). Luke also reports about the Woman with a Hemorrhage, who came up behind Jesus to touch the tassel on his cloak. Luke is specific about Jesus acknowledging "Some one *has touched* me; for I know *that power has gone out form me"* (Lk 8:46). Matthew and Mark report about people asking Jesus to allow them "to *touch* only the tassel on his cloak, and as many as *touched it* were healed" (Mt 14:36, Mk 6:56).

It is remarkable to note all these reports are about touching the tassel of Jesus in order to be healed. *Touching of the tassel* gives us an understanding of the effect of the sacramentals in the church. It is not the tassel per se that healed them, but the tassel of Jesus healed them. Sacramentals include objects like water, palms, and candles, medals, rosaries; places like the Holy

Land, grottoes, shrines; actions like blessings, laying of the hand to pray over the sick. More than things, places and actions, persons are more of a sacramental nature because they have Jesus within them. Human person is not to be reduced to a mere body; he or she is sacramental because of the Presence of Jesus in them.

There are other instances where Jesus touched the sick to heal them. Matthew records the healing of a leper. "He stretched out his hand, *touched* him." Matthew reports about the healing: "His leprosy was cleansed immediately" (Mt 8: 3,4). He *touched* the hand of Peter's mother-in-law and the fever left her (Mt 8:15). He *stretched out his hand* and caught him. This saved Peter from drowning into the sea (Mt 14:31). He *touched* the eyes of the two blind men, and their eyes were opened (Mt 9: 29). He *took the hand* of Jairus' daughter who was said to be dead, and the girl arose and walked around (Mk 5:41). He *put his finger* into man's ears and spitting, *touched* his tongue. The man's ears were opened; his speech impediment was removed (Mk 7: 33).

Jesus touched the sick to heal them. Jesus is not meant just for the people of His own time. It is because Jesus is the same yesterday, today, and forever (Heb 13: 8). He can be touched forever. He will touch the sick to heal forever. The "healing touch" was very much part of Jesus' formation of his Apostles. He summoned his Apostles to cure every disease and every illness during his ministry (Mt 10:1, Mk 6:7, Lk 9:1). They came back to report to Jesus about the healing touch they could give to the sick on His behalf. And after the Resurrection, as He was about to leave to go to his Father, He would summon them to lay hands on the sick to heal them (Mk 16:18). Luke reports that Jesus *raised his hands* and blessed them (Lk 24:50). Raising His hands to bless the Apostles was not meant only for the apostles, but for all who would be connected to his ministry. The action itself would be sacramental to bring the bread and wine into the body and blood of Jesus.

When a priest raises his hands to bless the bread and wine to turn them into the Body and Blood of Jesus, Jesus, the *sacrament* of healing, is present at the altar. And those who receive Jesus into them become the *sacramentals* of Jesus in the world. Thus continues in our lifetime the touch of Jesus. We can touch Jesus and He can touch us as we receive Jesus. As Liturgy professor Mark R. Francis puts it, "We are invited to experience God's love reaching out to us through our senses by means of everyday human actions. Our Sacramental viewpoint depends upon our sensitivity to God's grace at work in our everyday life."[2] In other words, when we receive the Lord into our body we use the sense of touch to touch the Lord. Thereby our bodies become the sacramentals, and all the actions present others with the healing touch.

My Personal Context:

My sensory experience especially that of the touch, is to reach out to others. It derives its power from the very presence of Jesus reaching out to others and me. He privileges me so that I can touch Him in the Eucharist. Everyone who receives His Presence becomes the sacramental Presence to one another. I shall heed the insight of St. Ephrem: "Christ's body has been mingled with our bodies, his blood too has been poured out into our veins, his voice in our ears, his brightness in our eyes. In his compassion the whole of Him has been mingled in with the whole of us."[3] These words inspire us to know that we are the sacramental Presence of the Lord for others.

Meditation:

After the preparatory steps:

I am conscious of His Presence in me, so that I can be His healing touch to others. I shall reach out to those who are suffering with whatever I can give. Whatever I give to ease the suffering is done with the consciousness of Christ in me reaching out to them. Let me be conscious of the one who asked me for prayers. Let me pray: *Lord Jesus I thank you for having mingled within me to make me your presence to the suffering. Lord, reach out to this particular person (name) who is in need of your healing touch. I thank you for touching her(him). I shall tell them what the Psalmist said:*

227

The Lord is close to the brokenhearted,
saves those whose spirit is crushed(34:19).

36. I Reach Out to the Victims of Natural Disasters

> We do not wage war with evil in the name
> of an abstract concept of duty. We do the
> good, not because it is value or because of
> expediency, but because we owe it to God.
>
> Abraham J. Heschel[1]

The catastrophic earthquake of 7.0 magnitude killed more than 150,000 people on Jan 12 of 2010. The cry of the victims reached the ends of the world. The United States spearheaded the emergency relief services and there was an outpouring of love, help, support and prayers for the dead, injured, displaced victims. The devastation suffered by the people of Haiti is unimaginable. So also, the extraordinary generosity of American people and elsewhere in the world is remarkable.

Richie, one of the committed Pro-Life leaders, was in the rectory on January 15. I heard him say to the secretary, "I hope we can take a second collection for the poor people in Haiti." This is the true reaction of a Catholic who feels within himself to cry the victim's cry.

In the wake of this terrible tragedy, there were many different reactions. I would summarize them into four:

First, the category of people whose reaction is, "Not me, thank God-attitude." They would say, "It did not happen to me; not to my family; not to my country; and so I thank God." This way of thanks is the most selfish and crude way of thanking God. I remember, one time guiding a retreat of young novices in India. On one evening we had to sit around the tabernacle for prayer of praise and petition. One of the novices prayed this way: "*Lord while there are people who have been handicapped, I thank you for making me born perfect in body and mind. Help me to be a good instrument in your church.*" Though this type of prayer seems to have a good intention, I had to disagree with the prayer. At the end of the prayer service, I did call the novice and asked, "Imagine if a handicapped person were to be seated by you when you prayed that way. Will that not offend her?" I went on to tell all the novices any sort of prayer that compares the misfortunes of others thus to thank God cannot be a prayer. On the other hand, prayers should always include our concern for the suffering of others. Jesus denouncing the prayer of the Pharisee for his comparison of the Tax Collector (Lk 18: 9-14) should be a reminder not to fall into the "Not me-thank God- attitude."

The second category of people describes the disasters as the punishment from God. Does this reaction make any sense at all? How does one construe this as the punishment of God? What did the Haitians do to deserve this magnitude of punishment? Why punish the innocent people and the children? Does it make sense to have a God who is the origin of life exterminating the children? These and other questions will tell us about anthropomorphism. As we have already mentioned in the context of the children born handicapped in Chapter 34, the idea of punishment is a crude anthropomorphism, which is totally unacceptable to the truth of the revelation of Divine Perfection.

The third category are those who seize these disasters like tornado, flood, hurricane, tsunami, earthquake to laugh at the believers, and to mock an 'all-knowing God,' 'all-powerful God,' 'all-good God.' They pose the age-old questions: Is there a God? If there is one, is He willing to prevent these tragedies? If He is not, He is powerless! If He is able, but not willing He is cruel. If He is able and willing, and yet these things happen, then He is evil! Why should bad things happen to good people? If God is in the church, why did the churches collapse? If the bishops are God- sent, why didn't God spare them from being killed by the earthquake? These and other rhetoric are the ludicrous statements that echo the sneering of the chief priests and the scribes at Jesus on the Cross: "Aha! He saved others, he cannot save himself" (Mk 15:31, Lk 23:35). It is a pity those who mock God do not want to learn from what happened to Jesus after his death. If they cannot accept the reality of Resurrection, any explanation about evil will fall far short to convince the skeptics. Abraham J Heschel, the famous Theologian says, "Evil is not man's ultimate problem. Man's ultimate problem is his relation to God."[2] We move on with the sense of accepting evil as mystery and trust in a God of eternal life.

The fourth category of people reacts in such a way to rush to help the victims. This is what most Americans and other nations have done to alleviate the suffering of the people in Haiti. These are not interested in knowing the scientific explanation of why it happened; they are not interested in knowing who the victims are, if they are of our race, color and nationality. They pass over all these only to listen to the human cry. When they hear the cry of those afflicted, they are like Moses listening to God's call: "I have heard the affliction of my people…I have heard their cry…I know well what they are suffering" (Ex 3:8a). They are like the Prophet Jeremiah listening to God: "Listen! The cry of the daughter of my people, far and wide" (Jer 8:19). They listen to Jesus, "Give them some food yourselves" (Mt 14:16). From all these biblical occurrences, we can infer that these are the people whose hands are the hands of God to reach out to the victims.

Jesus Himself heard the cry of his disciples at the storm at sea: "Teacher, do you not care that we are perishing." His listening to the cry made him calm the storm (Mk 4: 38). The cry of the suffering is the cry of Jesus Himself as He Himself said, "Whatever you did for one of these brothers of mine, you did for me" (Mt 25:40). Jesus is now present in the Eucharist, and He hears the cry of each and every victim. While the power of the Eucharistic Presence moves the entire world to listen to the cry of the victims, it calls those who receive the Lord to reach out to the victims. As Pope Benedict XVI puts it: "Each celebration of the Eucharist makes sacramentally present the gift that the crucified Lord made of his life, for us and for the whole world."[3] In our participation in the Eucharist we owe to God for the gift of life we receive from the Presence of Jesus.

My Personal Context:

I am one of those who would listen to the cry of the victims. The victims may be in my family, or in the neighborhood, or in my parish, or in my area, or in my state or in my country, or in another country. Every victim is my own brother and sister because of participation in the Eucharistic sacrifice. The Eucharist connects me and others in the world. Let me resound within me Blessed Mother Theresa's insight of St. Paul's message: *"I live, no longer I, but Christ lives in me" (Gal.2: 20). Christ prays in me. Christ speaks in me. Christ looks through my eyes. Christ speaks through my words. Christ works with my hands. Christ walks with my feet. Christ loves with my heart."*

Meditation:

After the preparatory steps:

I am conscious of my connection with the needy and the suffering and I am compassionate to them. Let me ease their suffering in whatever way I can. Let me begin with my prayer right now by which the Lord connects me to this person (these people). Let me pray: *Lord, You who are a listener to the cry of the suffering of the victims are connected with him (her). Thank you Lord for making me responsible to reach out to ease the suffering. I shall tell all those who suffer to join the Psalmist to pray:*

> *You are my shelter; from distress your keep me;*
> *With safety your ring me round (32:7).*

37. I See My Tears Being Transformed

We have a God who Himself cries, whose
Sacred Heart is broken with sadness.

Archbishop Timothy M. Dolan[1]

*The tsunami that killed so many thousands of people in
Southeast Asia on Dec 26, 2004 is still a nightmare for many
people. India was worst hit by it. Vijayan, one of my cousins lost
his parents, his wife and children. He lost the entire family except
Karuna, his only sister. Sr. Karuna is a nun of the Order of
Grace and Compassion Sisters. Her convent is hundreds of miles
away from her village that was hit by the Tsunami. Vijayan
escaped because he had gone to a medical store to get the
prescriptions for his mother. When he returned, he saw his house
partially destroyed and all of the family killed in it. His first
reaction was crying to God, "O God you spared me! For what?"
His life without his parents, wife, and children was devastating.
He was walking around like a depressed man; crying aloud every
time someone met him.*

*Six years have passed by. He and his sister in the convent
have moved on with life's commitment. Sr.Karuna could move on
well as she is nun who gets the prayer-support from her
community sisters. It took many years for Vijayan to get back to
the normal life pattern. He began to realize the only way to keep*

235

moving was to take refuge in the Lord, and his tears have slowly changed into joy.

The cries of Vijayan and those of thousands of the victims of the Sept 11 attack, hurricane and all other disasters, echo the cries of the Book of Lamentation: "Worn out from weeping are my eyes, within me all is in ferment." The "within me" experience of the cry was going to take a different experience as Jesus Himself would be present "within" the victims. The Incarnation made it possible for all of us to have God within us. And so Jesus cries within us when we go through devastating experiences. Jesus would teach this saying, "Blessed are you who are now weeping, for you will laugh" (Lk 6:21b).

Jesus cried. The Gospels mentions at least three places where Jesus cried. He wept over Jerusalem (Lk 19:41). He cried at the death of Lazarus (Jn 11:35). And Jesus cried at the cross (Lk 23:46). These moments of Jesus' weeping gave rise to transformation of divine power. The weeping of Jesus was not the sign of weakness. On the contrary, it points out something of a transformational power.

Jesus wept over Jerusalem because of his foresight of the destruction of the temple of Jerusalem. It did happen in 70 A.D by the Romans. But the weeping was transformed to foresee the formation of the Church, which no one can destroy. We see four transformational characters.

First, People in Jerusalem did not recognize Jesus as Messiah. But St. Peter's confession recognized Jesus as Messiah and it would establish the Church (Mt 16:16). The Greek word for Church, *Ekklesia* does not refer to a building, but to God's people. *Jerusalem* here does not refer to the city but to the community of people in Jerusalem. They failed to confess Jesus as their Messiah, but on the same confession there would emerge the community of believers, the church. Second, the destruction is of the temple. On the contrary, the Church will be the Body of the Risen Christ in whom the believers become one with him. Third is an interesting observation about the word *Kepa* that means *rock*. This is transliterated into Greek as *Cephas* and translated into Greek as *Petros,* meaning *movable stone* or *Petra* meaning *unmovable stone*. The English translation is, "You are Peter (Petros) and upon this rock (Petra) I will build my church." In Jesus' saying- "There will not be one stone left upon another…"(Mk 13:2)- the stones (petros, the movable stones) of the temple will be moved and destroyed by the enemies. On the contrary, the church, i.e. the community of believers, will be built on Petra, the rock that is unmovable or unconquerable by the enemies. Fourth, in contrast to the enemies' power to destroy the city and the temple, "the gates of the netherworld shall not prevail against it" (Mt 16:18). No power of enemies can destroy the Church, the Body of the Risen Christ. Thus we see the

237

weeping of Jesus was transformed into the power of the Church-*the community of God's people*-that will never be destroyed or conquered.

The weeping at the death of Lazarus was transformed into the power of bringing him back to life. The weeping at the cross did end with the death, but was transformed into the Resurrection of Jesus. St. Paul understands the power of resurrection as God raising His Son "to put all things beneath his feet and gave him as head over all things to the church, which is his body, the fullness of the one whom fills all things in every way"(Eph 1: 22-23). Every believer becomes part of Christ's Body. That is why St. Paul tells us, " Now you are Christ's body, and individually parts of it"(1Cor 12: 27). Christ is mystically present within every believer in the church, and as St. Paul says, "If one part suffers, all the parts suffer with it" (1Cor12:26a). Christ Himself suffers within a believer, and cries within him or her.

The cry of Jesus within the victims should not be taken as inability or incapability. The Lord is within that person to take upon the suffering and to guide the person to the transformational effects. Those transformational effects will not be taken away as it is guaranteed by his indwelling Presence. This is what the church has witnessed in countless numbers of her members.

The Presence of Jesus in the Eucharist tells us the same consoling words of the Last Supper Discourses (Chapters of Jn

14-16). We can listen to these: *Do not let your hearts be troubled. You have faith in God; have faith also in me (14:1) and we will come to make our dwelling with you (14:23b). Remain in my love (15:9b). You will grieve, but your grief will become joy (16:20b). In the world you will have trouble, but take courage, I have conquered the world (16:33b).* These words are reminiscent of His words of comfort to the suffering during His life on earth. They have eternal value to all of us.

My Personal Context:

When I struggle with my suffering, I am like Job of the OT. He became the victim of different devastating experiences. Like Job, I will never give up hope because I know my savior still lives. He lives in the Eucharist. From the Eucharist, He comes to dwell within me. In all the circumstances of sickness, distress, disasters, accidents, death, I know I am never alone to face the suffering. Jesus is within me, struggling and crying within me to transform my suffering into His power.

Meditation:

After the preparatory steps:

I am conscious of Jesus coming into me. I encounter the present suffering (......) Along with me, my Savior Jesus cries within me. My cries are mystically one with that of Jesus. My suffering is being transformed into His Power. Let me pray: *Thank You Jesus for being within me. Your power has helped me to move on with my life. I am joyful, and I believe nothing will take away my joy. And so let me sing with the Psalmist*

The Lord lives! Blessed be my rock!

Exalted be God, my Savior! (18:47).

Notes:
Chapter 34
1. Albert Nolan, *Jesus today,* (NY: Orbis books, 2006), p.117.
2. Didache-Web: "Church Fathers," translation of J.B.Lightfoot.
3. Ronald Rolheiser, *Against and infinite horizon,* (NY: Crossword Publishing Co.1995), p.147.
Chapter 35
1. John Powel.S.J, *Will the real me please stand up?* (Allen TX: RCL, 1985), p.165.
2. Mark.R. Francis, C.S.V, and Article: *Have sacraments changed?* Web: An American cathoilc.org/Cathoilic Update.
3. Cited from Owen F Cummings, *Eucharistic Doctors.* (NJ: Paulist Press, 2005), p.46.
Chapter 36
1. Abraham J. Heschel, *God in search of man,* (NY: Farrar, Straus and Giroux, 1955), p.376.
2. Ibid., p. 376.
3. Benedict XVI, *The Sacrament of charity,* (Washington, D.C.: USCCB Publishing, #7), p. 74.
Chapter 37
1. Timothy M. Dolan, *From why to how to whom in Haiti* (Catholic New York, Jan 28, 2010) #10

VIII. My Resource

38. I Go to the House of God

The mass, The Eucharist, is the coming
together of the people of God made
present now in our time.

Basil Pennington[1]

In 2005, I was invited to preach a three day retreat for a group of college professors in India. It was an inspiring three days for me and for them. The main theme was the Mystical Presence of God in our day to day life. After the retreat, one of the professors came up with something which I shall paraphrase: " All these three days we have been meditating on the Mystical Presence of Jesus in each of us; now that it is clear that God is within me, should I go to Church at all? We are also told in the Bible that God does not live in the house built by hands. Isn't it all the more reason why we need not have to go to church to experience God?" This raised the eyebrows of all, and they were all looking at me to answer him. Probably everyone seemed to go with his logic. I was able to answer this question, and some of what was said to them at that time will be the contents of this chapter.

First, we should read any text of the Bible in its context. We cannot take it out of context to prove what we want to prove. *Context* includes the place, time, people, thinking, belief, culture, circumstances, etc. For example, the context of this text- *"The*

God who made the world and all that is in it, the Lord of heaven and earth, does not dwell in sanctuaries made by human hands"(Acts 17:24)- is St. Paul preaching in Areopagus, which is the cultural center of that time. Paul debates the Greek pagan practices of having temples for gods and goddesses. Their belief was such they could contain a particular god or goddess in their temples. Paul wanted to educate them into their new thinking that God is omnipresent; Christ, the Son of God is the true God of man's salvation. Paul would look at an altar dedicated to "an unknown god", and present Christ as the Unknown God to them. Yet they were told not to limit Christ to a place. This context in no way goes against the Eucharistic Presence of Christ in the churches.

Second, any interpretation should take into account the revelation of God' plan to send His own Son to dwell among us for the salvation of mankind. All the interpretations should draw inspiration from the reference to Christ' Birth, Life, Death and Resurrection, and lead us to His Presence. For example, in the early church people wanted to kill Stephen who preached the salvation in Christ over Moses and the practices of the temple of Jerusalem. The context is that the people who had accepted the Temple of Jerusalem as the place of worship would, at the same time, reject Christ, the Lord. So Stephen would come and declare, "The Most high does not dwell in houses made by human hands"

(Acts 7:48). Again, Stephen's words should not be taken out of context; rather it is the manifestation of Stephen's faithful reference to Christ's Presence for our salvation.

Third, salvation of mankind is not an ideology but an experience. This began with Christ here on earth, lived and continued here on earth, with the hope of fulfillment in eternal life. The gradual unfolding of God's plan to have the covenant with the people to be in their midst came to a fulfillment when Jesus, the Son of God, became flesh to dwell among us in the world. Jesus by His Resurrection became Christ to be present all over the world, especially with His presence with us in the church for the nourishment of our life on earth. Eucharistic Presence in the church is the legacy of Christ's promise to be with us till the end of the world.

God's covenant: *"Ever present in your midst, I will be your God, and you will be my people" (Lev 26:12)* made the OT people build the tent to be known "Dwelling with its tent" (Ex 35:11,36:8). People did see the Ark of the Covenant, which was understood, as God's Presence with them in the tent. Gradually Salomon wanted to build the temple for God according to the plan revealed by God (1Kg 8:15). Yet he realized with his wisdom that the omnipresent God couldn't be contained in the Temple: "Can it indeed be that God dwells among men? If the heavens and the highest heavens cannot contain you, how much less this temple which I have built?" (1Kg 8:27). And so people would profess that Heavens are His thrones and Earth is His footstool (Is 66:1). And the Temple would be considered the resting place for his feet (Ps 99: 5). People would say, "Let us enter God's dwelling; let us worship at God's footstool" (Ps 132:7), and they would cry out to God, "Arise Lord, come to your resting place, you and your majestic ark" (132:9).

Church does not mean the building; neither can it limit His Presence. It is the place where people who have been redeemed to be the Body of Christ can continue to gather to be nourished by Christ abiding presence in the Eucharist. The ancestors of Jesus would go to the mountain to pray; then the Temple of Jerusalem was there to pray and to offer the sacrifices. Even after building the temple, mountains remained always part of the people's experience to worship God It is remarkable to note that John the Baptist, who prepared the way for Jesus, would say the "mountains and hills shall be made low." And people did not have to walk through the "winding roads" and "rough ways" to go to the mountain to pray. All will see the salvation of God in Jesus.

Jesus Himself, who knew the relevance of mountain, went to pray (Mk 6:48). When the time came He revealed to the Samaritan woman, "Believe me, woman, the hour is coming when you will worship the Father neither on the mountain nor in

Jerusalem." "Jerusalem" here denotes the Temple. At the cleansing of the temple he would reveal He is the Temple in the Temple itself: "Destroy this temple and in three days I will raise it up" (Jn 2:19). Obviously it is a reference to His Resurrection that would make Him the Temple. After the Resurrection the communities of believers are the church, as they have become members of His body (Eph1:23). The believers said, "We are the temple of the living God" (2Cor 6:16). The very conviction being the temple of God made the first Christians to gather together in houses. As the number increased, they devoted themselves to meeting together in the temple area to worship (cf. Acts 2:46, 47). So the 'Church' does not just refer to the building of the church. It is experienced as New Heaven and the New Earth: "Behold, God's dwelling is with the human race" (Rev 21:3).

My Personal Context:

I realize that going to church is not being in the building. As the word 'Temple' has assumed marvelous meanings in the course of salvation history, I too am one with the transformation effected in me through Christ, the Temple. My body has become the temple; I have become part of the Church, the Temple. The building of the church houses the Dwelling of the living God in Jesus, though God is not limited nor contained in it. I am connected with the living Presence of Jesus, whose Presence connects me with my eternal home.

Meditation:

After the preparatory steps:

Christ's omnipresence in the church can reach every one. He has come into me. Now I have become the living temple as Christ is living within me. I am renewed to be the living member of Christ's Body. In and through me the new covenant is being fulfilled. I shall go to church until I dwell in the House of God forever in the Heavenly Jerusalem. *Let me pray: Let me be mystically connected with You all the time. Let me thank you for your Eucharistic Presence that connects me with every one in Heaven and Earth. Let me rejoice with the Psalmist:*

I rejoiced when they said to me,

"Let us go to the house of the Lord"(122:1).

39. I Am Close to Jesus in the Church

God is closer to me than I am to myself: my being depends upon
God's being near to me and present to me.

Meister Eckhart[1]

*Sacristans in the church, I think, after that of the priests,
are so privileged to be close to the Eucharistic Presence. Richard
and Elizabeth, a devoted couple, are sacristans in St. Mary's,
Wappingers Falls. Richard and Elizabeth keep track of all the
things in the sacristy connected with the liturgical seasons. They
set up all that is necessary for the daily noon mass. As
extraordinary Eucharistic ministers they are devoted to the
Eucharist, and Richard is also one of the Lectors, familiar with
the Gospel stories. When I reminded them of the Gospel story of
Simeon and Anna, who wanted to see and be close to the Savior
at the Temple of Jerusalem, they humbly acknowledged, "It is a
privilege to do these services; and we are blessed to be close to
altar of God."*

*Ray, another sacristan, has been doing this service on
Sundays for more than 15 years. He says, "I consider this a
privilege and blessing to be of service to priests and the church."*

*Like Richard and Elizabeth and Ray, there are many
thousands of people who volunteer to do church activities without
expecting anything in return.*

We think of the very origin of our lives, we are created in His image and likeness. And so, every human being has a longing to see and experience God. It is like humans cannot but have the capacity for thinking; so also humans cannot but have the longing for God. St. Augustine grasped this inner longing to say it well: "You have made us for yourself, O Lord, and our hearts are restless until they rest in you" (Confessions 1,1). The longing for God is an indispensable capacity of every human being, including the atheists and agnostics. No one can deny this.

Man's longing for God is evidenced in salvation history. We can sense this longing in the very curiosity and longing of Moses to go over to look at the burning bush more closely. But God said, "Come no nearer!"(Ex 3: 5). And the longing of other people *to meet God* is another example where Moses called them to come to the foot of the mountain. God came down to the people in the cloud around the mountain; yet the people were warned not to touch even the base of the mountain (Ex 19:12). The longing of the people *to worship God* at the foot of the mountain was witnessed in their life. God told them, "You shall all worship at some distance, but Moses alone is to come close to the Lord; the others shall not come too near, and the people shall not come up at all with Moses"(Ex 24: 1,2). People's longing was also witnessed in their wrong move to make them a god in the golden calf (cf. Ex 32). It was the sign of human longing to see and touch God.

Unlike the OT experience of people at the mountain, where they could not be close to God's presence, the incarnation of God in Jesus brought about a complete reversal, where God Himself becomes man not only to be close to us, but also to be within us. St. John looks at the very wonder of the Word becoming flesh to make his dwelling among us. He has a sense of fulfillment to say that we *saw* His glory (Jn 1: 14), and exclaims, "No one has ever seen God. The only son, God who is at the Father's side, has revealed him" (Jn 1:18). John is very descriptive of the sense experience in the prologue for his first letter: "what we have heard, what we have seen with our eyes, what we looked upon and touched with our hands" (1Jn 1: 1). John's experience is indicative of the quest of people who longed to be close to God.

The Gospels tell us about the experience of the crowd to long for that fulfillment: the great crowd *to follow* Jesus (Mt 8:1), to *gather around him* (Mk 4: 1,5:21), *to touch him* (Mk 6: 56), *to listen* to him (Lk 21: 38). And there are stories of individual experience of the longing. Experience like a leper *approaching* him for healing (Mt 8: 2); a sinful woman *weeping and bathing his* feet with her tears (Lk 7: 38); Jairus *falling at his feet* to ask for healing for his daughter (Mk 5: 22); a woman with hemorrhage *touching his cloak* (Mk 5: 27); Mary *sitting at his feet to listen* to him (Lk 11:39) are remarkable stories of individual experiences of being close to Jesus.

At the last supper, the longing of both God and man- *the incarnation of Jesus to be with us and the humans to be close to God-* were coming to a perfect fulfillment. The preparations for the Last Supper bring down to us the preparations we do at all the churches for the sacrifice of the mass. The discourse at the table on the vine and the branches is the remarkable union and the closeness we enjoy at the Eucharist. The farewell prayer known as The High Priestly Prayer, especially-*I wish where I am they also be with me-* renders the eternal bond we have in the Eucharist. Eating the Bread, and drinking the cup is the pledge of our eternal banquet. All these are reminiscences of the closeness of God and man.

Archbishop Fulton Sheen builds up a logical construct to argue that in the Eucharist human longing finds its fulfillment: "If human love craves oneness, shall not divine love? If husband and wife seek to be one in the flesh, shall not the Christian and Christ crave for that oneness with one another?...Every heart seeks a happiness outside it and since perfect love is God, then the heart of man and the heart of Christ must, in some way, fuse. In human friendship the other person is loved as another self, or the other half of ones soul. Divine friendship must have its mutual *indwelling*: "He who dwells in love dwells in God and God in him" (1Jn 4: 7). This aspiration of the soul for its ecstasy is fulfilled in the Sacrament of the Eucharist"[2]

My Personal Context:

Even today I long within myself, "if only I had lived during the time of Jesus…? Sometimes I long within myself, "if only I am fortunate to have Christ appearing to me…? I can now understand that these are my longings to be close to Him. As St. John Chrysostom says, "You do see him, touch him, eat him!…He gives himself to you, not merely to look upon, but even to touch, to eat and to receive within you."[3] My participation at every Eucharistic celebration is an experience where my longing to be close to Him is being realized, and so, let me be more conscious than ever before of my closeness to Christ.

Meditation:

After the preparatory steps:

I am conscious at my deepest level of my closeness to Jesus. I have become one with Him. Let me glorify Him in my body in all what I say and do. Let me pray: *Lord Jesus, You are within me. I can never ask for more than to be close to you. May this closeness be with me till I am with you forever? Let me pray with the Psalmist:*

> *How lovely your dwelling,*
> *O Lord of hosts!*

My soul yearns and pines
for the courts of the lord.
My heart and flesh cry out
for the living god (Ps 84:2,3).

40. I Consecrate Every Day with His Presence

Every day of life more and more increases
my gratitude to God for having made me
what I am.

St Elizabeth Seton[1]

Fr. Rajan, my friend and classmate, is the parochial vicar of St. Elizabeth Ann Seton parish, Shrub Oak. At one time when I asked him to take me to JFK Airport, he was unable to do so because of his pastoral responsibilities. He asked Denis, one of his parishioners, to take me to the Airport. Denis was very pleasant from the first moment of his driving. The trip took about an hour. Denis' conversation touched upon his visit to Madjugoria in November of 1996. He traveled with his wife Joann. Their conversion story took place during that visit. Their conversion was from their 'nominal' Catholic life to 'a practicing and believing' Catholic life.

The conversion was such that they came to really believe in the real presence of Jesus in the Eucharist. Ever since that experience, daily mass became the center of their lives. Denis says, "Daily participation at the mass opens up my heart, to take to Jesus, not only my worries, but of others and of the world, and at the end of the mass I feel better. Joann added, "I don't want to live my days without the Eucharist; one day without the Eucharist makes me so empty; Jesus is everything for me."

There are many daily communicants like Denis and Joann, whose daily life is consecrated every day. No day is taken for granted when it is valued in the Presence of God. It is probable that their conviction is fashioned after that of Archbishop Dolan who says, "That we here would have God's own life within us fanned into a flame through our participation in the Eucharist first thing each morning is a genuine blessing, one that would, God willing, be a source of joy all through the day."[2]

For ancient Israel, a day was considered to begin with sunset and to cover a 24-hour time from sunset to sunset. The creation story of the Book of Genesis presents the creative activity of God at work for six days and rest on the seventh day. It was to revere the sacredness of the Sabbath rest that began by sunset on Friday to sunset on Saturday. In the course of the life of the people of Israel, the Sabbath day, its sacredness and the observances, determined the activities of all other six days. On the Sabbath day, the people of Israel would remember not only the creation of God but also all the marvelous deeds God had done for them. Remembering God, sharing the meal, having rest, would renew their body, mind and spirit to continue their work for the following six days. In other words, *their worship of the living God on the Sabbath would bless them in their day to day work and their living.*

In the Hebrew calendar, Sunday was considered the first day of the week. All four Gospels report that the resurrection of Jesus took place "on the first day of the week" (Mt 28:1, Mk 16:2, Lk 20:1, Jn 20:1). And so, the early Christians came together to commemorate the Resurrection of the Lord on the first day of the week. The power of the Resurrection of Jesus brought the first Christians together almost every day (Acts 2:42-47). They combined the custom of breaking the bread with their gathering on the first day of the week. Initially the breaking of the bread was the common meal shared by the believers as reported in the Acts of the Apostles: "On the first day of the week when they gathered to break bread" (Acts 20:1). As St. Paul records it, (1Cor 11:23-28) gradually the remembrance of the Lord's Supper and the Eucharistic sharing of the bread and wine would replace the breaking of the bread. Thus "breaking of the bread" would henceforth refer to the Eucharistic celebration.

"The first day of the week" would soon be known as the Lords Day. Revelation of John written around AD 81-96 mentions it as "the Lord's Day" (Rev 1:10). The early Christian writings of Didache, the letters of St. Ignatius of Antioch, St. Ireaneus and St. Justin bear witness to the celebration of the Eucharist on the *Lord's day*. St. Ignatius, who lived between ca 35 to 110, writes, "…. Let every friend of Christ keep the Lords Day as a festival, the resurrection- day, the queen of all the days"(Letter to Magnasinas 9).[3] And St.Justin, who lived between ca 100-165, is the first Christian writer to use the name *Sunday*. In his First Apology-67, "on the day called Sunday, all who live in cities or in the country gather together to one place."[4] Like the Sabbath day observance sanctified the rest of the week, the worship of the First day of the week became the norm of worship to sanctify the rest of the days of the week. *It is because the Eucharist made a profound sense of sacredness to their daily life.*

In the early Christian communities, every day was considered sacred. Every evening was like dying with Christ and every morning rising with Christ. This was probably inspired by St. Paul's understanding of a Christian "dying and rising" with Jesus in our Baptism (cf. Rom 6:3, 4). Every day was devoted to the Eucharist in the early Christian communities. St. Ignatius in his letter to the Romans described Eucharistic strength summoning them from the rising of the sun to the setting of the sun: "How good it is to be sinking down below the world's horizon towards God, to rise again later into the dawn of his presence."[5] *Thus we witness the unfolding of God's plan to have the Eucharistic Presence in our daily life: "we will live, and move and have our being"(Acts 17:28).* This is the early Christian experience of the Eucharist. The profound longing to have the daily Eucharist is seen already by the beginning of the third century. St. Cyprian, who lived c 200-258, writes, "Moreover we ask that this bread be given daily."[6] St. Ambrose, who lived C339-373 writes, "Receive daily what is benefit to you daily."[7] By the seventh century, daily Eucharistic celebrations were part of the monasteries. Then the parishes began to have daily Eucharistic celebrations. Now that the Eucharist is celebrated every day all over the world, everyone has the opportunity to sanctify our daily life rather than to wait for Sunday. Drawing from the experience of the OT Sabbath and the NT Sunday, all of us can sanctify our lives daily with His Presence in the Eucharist.

My Personal Context:

Each and every day is a gift to me. Every day I rise with Him to new life. Every day is my awakening to His Presence. May Benedict Groeschel's prayer becomes my personal prayer: "I look at the tabernacle, towards its glowing candles. Your shining presence there invites me to a new day, to start afresh. Your love in giving me your Eucharistic presence-which is just as real as your presence at Nazareth-fills me with great confidence as the day begins. I ask you to come with me when I leave the church, when duty and responsibility call me forth to begin the day. I ask you to be the unseen presence in all that I do." [8]

Meditation:

After the preparatory steps:

I am all the more conscious of His Presence within me. In Him I live, move and have my being. His Presence within me sanctifies my daily life. Let this day begin (be guided) with His Presence. Let me pray: *Lord God I praise you for being with me. I realize more than ever before that you never leave me, even if I were to forget your Presence within me: I shall praise you with the psalmist:*

> *Only goodness and love will pursue me*
> *all the days of my life;*
> *I will dwell in the house of the LORD*
> *for years to come (23:6).*

41. I Am a Member of the Body of Christ

The organic oneness of the human family
achieved still greater unity by being
incorporated into God's Son through his
incarnation and resurrection.

Thomas Keating[1]

*Andrew and Kathleen, a devoted couple to the Eucharist,
are Eucharistic ministers. Their son, commonly known as 'AJ', is
a young teenaged, talented singer, who cantors from the choir
loft on Sundays. His sister Brianna joins him in the choir loft. It
happens that on certain Sundays the Eucharistic ministers don't
go up to the choir loft to distribute communion to the choir
members. On those Sundays, without fail, Andrew or Kathleen
would come to me at the end of the mass with a humble request if
I could give communion to their son and daughter. This has
always edified me.*

*Asked about this faith of Andrew and his wife for their
enthusiasm for the Eucharist, Andrew attributes that to his
parents. He says, "My parents' faith in the Eucharist has a
tremendous influence on me. They would never be happy if I were
to miss the Eucharist at mass; even if there were minor things in
my way, I would always make peace within me to receive the
Eucharist. That would bring peace within me. And it is my turn
now to tell my kids not to miss receiving the Eucharist."*

261

Andrew and Kathleen are wonderful examples of many young couples in the Church who are devoted to the Eucharist. Their devotion goes beyond their individual reception of the Eucharist. They are also interested in other members of the family to be connected to the Eucharist. The participation of each family at the Eucharist- that unites each member of the family into one family- becomes the blessing for other families.

The story of Mankind's First Family is before us. The book of Genesis tells us about the first 'blaming.' Adam blamed Eve for sin (Gen 3:12). Then we are told about the first 'enmity' between the brothers, Cain and Abel (Gen 4:8). And, we are told about the vulnerability of freedom, by which Cain could ask God, "Am I my brother's keeper?"(Gen.4:9). All the possible finger pointing, blaming, enmities, misuse of freedom etc, that are part of some of our families were implied in the story of the first family of salvation history. God educated the family members first, to remain united to Him in their lives. God's own initiative to make the covenant with Noah *"to bless him and his sons"* (Gen 9:1) is the prototype of all the families that would be united to God. God's covenant with Abraham, *"All the communities of the earth shall find blessing in you"* (Gen 12:3b) is another prototype of families. Here the union with God would become the blessing to all other communities.

'Union' with God is to be drawn to the Holiness of God. The Holiness of God is a demanding one: *Be holy for I, the Lord, your God, am holy* (Lev 19:2). Holiness is the very foundation of families. All the other conducts and behaviors depend on this foundation. Everyone in the family becomes responsible for the other. Holiness of God would demand, for instance, "You shall not bear hatred for your brother in your heart"(Lev 19:17a)."You shall love your neighbor as yourself" (Lev 19: 17b). The Holiness of God would require the parents to teach their children: "Therefore, you shall love the Lord, your God, with all your heart, and with all your soul, and with all your strength. Take to heart these words which I enjoin on you today. Drill them into your children. Speak of them at home and abroad, whether you are busy or rest" (Dt 6: 5-7). All these 'holy' responsibilities emerge from the union with God. These responsibilities all the more strengthen each member of the family to be united to God. Jesus, the Son of God, would make them become part of His own Body.

At the institution of the Eucharist, during his farewell discourse, Jesus makes clear the ultimate goal of the Eucharist. Jesus said, "They may all be one, as you, Father, are in me and I in you, that they also may be in us, That the world may believe that you sent me" (Jn 17:21). Jesus brings in the realistic *metaphor* of the Vine and the Branches. Metaphors are of human experience by which He introduces His own experience. Jesus takes the metaphor of Vine and its branches to tell us about His union with the Father, and His intention of this metaphor is meant for us to find our union in them. Each family can find this metaphor realistic as it reflects their own families. Each family is like vine and branches. The parents being the Vine have their children as the branches. Jesus, the Eucharist, is the Vine; we the families are the branches united with him. All the families become one Body of Christ in and through the Eucharist.

St. Paul, realizing the efficacy of our union with Jesus tells us that we are members of one Body: "so we, though many, are one body in Christ and individually parts of one another" (Rom 12:5; refer also 1Cor 12:12). Paul calls this union "the church" (Eph 1:23), because we have become one Body of Christ on earth. 'Church' here does not refer to a place or a thing but a realistic experience of union. St. Augustine takes this teaching of St. Paul seriously to tell us, "You hear the words of "The Body of Christ" and you reply "Amen." Be then, a member of Christ's body, so that your Amen may accord with the truth."[2] This union is what makes us the Body of Christ. And so, now we have the 'Communion,' with Jesus. In the Eucharist, we have 'communion' with Christ, and so we are the Body of Christ.

By becoming the Body of Christ, we become the chosen ones to be the blessings to others. As we have seen the covenant with Abraham-*all the communities of the earth shall find blessing in you*-now becomes true of all the chosen families. It is because the New Covenant in Jesus cannot be limited to just one family. Each family that is united to Jesus now, in the words of Pope Benedict XVI, has to "embrace all the world." The Pope says, "The Eucharistic community-within which all of us receiving the same Lord become one body and embrace all the world."[4] It means every family united to Jesus becomes the blessings to all the communities. The blessings are mystical in effect. The blessing of love, peace, and forgiveness embraces the entire world in and through us. This is again, the 'holy responsibility' God gave to the chosen families.

The "union" we have, and the "blessing" we are for others, have been part of our own families. At home, we who eat food at the family table together witness the union and blessing of the family members. The same union is witnessed at every celebration of the Eucharist. We can tangibly see the manifestation of this union as everyone receives the same Communion.

My Personal Context:

The experience of union has come down to me from my own parents. My family is the greatest sign of my union with one another in the Church. I with my family make up the branch; the branch cannot survive without the Vine, the body of Jesus. Let me remind myself of what Jesus tells me, "whoever remains in me and I in him will bear much fruit" (Jn 15:5b). One of the fruits is that we, as families, become the blessings for other families in the Eucharistic community.

Meditation:

After the preparatory steps:

I am conscious of my union with one another. This day I would like to be more aware of the Eucharist that enables me to be united to all. We make the Body of Christ. It is the fruit of my union with Christ. And so, let me pray: *Lord Jesus I thank you for coming into me. Help me to acknowledge that you are within all who receive you in the Eucharist. Help me to appreciate this inter-connectedness I have with each other till we are all united with you forever. Let me join the Psalmist to praise your marvelous plan of bringing all of us together:*

How good it is, how pleasant,
Where the people dwell as one! (133:1).

42. I Pray for Others in the Eucharistic Presence

> Some people think that religion comes
> about as a perception of an answer to a
> prayer, while in truth it comes about in our
> knowing that God shares our prayer.
>
> Abraham J. Heschel[1]

Susan, one of our lectors and a devoted parishioner, sent an email asking the rectory secretary, Mary Ann, to ask the priests for special prayers for her daughter Maria. Here below is the exact copy of the email.

Hi Mary Ann,

Maria will be taking her last Final Exam tomorrow in Pathology, and I didn't find out in time to put her in the parish book of intentions. Could you please ask Monsignor and Father Dhas to put a word for her with The Boss and may be St. Jude, too, for good measure…this one is going to be really hard, and she needs at least a C to officially graduate. Thanks!..Susan

Of course, prayers worked. Maria passed the exam.

Ralph, another parishioner, has a unique habit as he enters to the Church. He goes to the Book of Intentions to write the intention. Asked why he does it all the time, he answered "I come to church to pray. That is why I go right there to write various intentions, mainly for world peace.

Susan for her daughter and Ralph for world peace reflect the mind of thousands and thousands of Catholics who believe in the power of prayer.

The salvation history has lots of insights about the power of prayer. 'Prayer' has taken many forms in the course of the history of mankind. The salvation history clarifies the very concept of prayer, which is so vast that we can never contain enough within a chapter. We shall have a glimpse of it in the context of the Eucharist. As we are aware, more than ever before, the Presence of Jesus in the Eucharist has made a tremendous impact on believers to pray.

One cannot understand the power of prayer without understanding God's goodness that initiates humans to pray. Prophet Isaiah reports about God's initiative to deliver the people of Israel. He also remarks about the indifference of the same people. That made God to say, "Why did no one answer when I called?" (Is 50:2). God Himself would go ahead with His initiative to help them in spite of their non-response. God said, "I was ready to respond to those who asked me not, to be found by those who sought me not. I said, Here I am! Here I am! To a nation that did not call upon my name" (Is 65: 1). Prayer is *first the initiative of God saying to us "Here I am"* It is God who initiates first to communicate with us for our sake. We are free to respond to God's initiative.

There are many examples of men responding to God's initiative. Let us take the examples of Moses and Samuel. God first took the initiative to deliver the people from the land of Egypt. He called Moses. Moses responded, "Here I am" (Ex 3:4). There is the dramatic story of Samuel. God takes the initiative to establish the kingdom of David. He called Samuel. Samuel responded, "Here I am" (1Sam 3:4). These stories of the responses of Moses and Samuel give us an idea of prayer. Moses was called to go up to the Mountain to have the experience of prayer. Samuel was there in the Temple to have the experience of prayer. Prayer becomes *the meeting point of the "Here I am" of God and the "Here I am" of man.*

With the New Testament begins the divine initiative and the human response in the person of Jesus. Jesus becomes the meeting point of God and man. The sending of His own Son is the "Here I am-initiative" of God. St. John tells us of the initiative- *"He was in the world"*-but the world did not accept him (Jn 1:11). Yet God did not relinquish His initiative to save mankind. Yet the humans were free to respond to His presence. But to those who did accept Him, He gave power to become children of God (Jn 1:12). Here again, the response of the children of God is not of human decision but of God. St John says, "they were born not by natural generation nor by human choice nor by a man's decision but of God" (Jn 1:13). It is God's initiative to send His own Son. By accepting Jesus, we respond to God' initiative to pray through Jesus, in Jesus, and with Jesus. Jesus is the meeting point. Prayer is no more the privilege of certain individuals like Moses and Samuel. All those who have become the children are privileged to respond in prayer as the meeting point in Jesus.

Since Jesus is the meeting point of prayer, He corrected some of their ways of praying, and finally taught them how to pray. The first and the most important insight is prayer has to do not with one individual as it was thought of in the Old Testament, but with all who have accepted His initiative. God is no more "my" Father, but "Our" Father. It is not "I" as an individual, but all of us, "His children" responding to Him. "Our Father in heaven, hallowed be your name, your kingdom come, your will be done on earth as in heaven" is about "our" response to praise the initiative of God. And the rest of the prayer is all about presenting the needs of one another in prayer. In other words, we, His children are in a privileged position like Moses and Samuel to pray for others in the world. Jesus would make the meeting point of God and us in the institution of His Presence in the Eucharist.

At the Last Supper discourse, after the institution of the Eucharist, Jesus was addressing the crisis of the disciples who would not have his bodily presence. Jesus promised them the

Holy Spirit. It is again another initiative of God: "And I will ask the Father, and he will give you another Advocate to be with you always, the Spirit of truth" (Jn 14:16). In the absence of His bodily presence, His Spirit becomes the power to unite all men and women to Jesus by indwelling in all. This is again God's initiative that *His Spirit indwelling in all, and connecting all to pray.* St. Paul too affirms "God sending the spirit of his Son into our hearts, crying out, "Abba, Father!"(Gal 4: 6).

The Eucharistic Lord has not only become the person for us to pray, but also the meeting point of prayer. When we assemble in His Presence, each of us is moved by the Spirit to be connected to all the children of God. The indwelling of the Holy Spirit is experienced in our inmost being. As Thomas Keating puts it, "As one moves into his own inmost being, he comes into contact with the inmost being of everyone else. Although each of us retains his own unique personhood, we are necessarily associated with the God-man, who has taken the whole family to himself in such a way as to be the inmost reality of each individual member of it."[3] Each of us has the inmost realm. Holy Spirit in the inmost makes us transcend our own individual self to be connected to all. Here begins our prayer for one another. Thus Eucharist remains the eternal initiative of God for us to be united to Him to pray for one another.

My Personal Context:

God's initiative is always before me. The spirit of the Risen Christ within me makes me respond to God and say, "Here I am." In His Presence in the Eucharist, I am with Jesus. I am in Jesus because the Spirit is within me. Through Him, I pray with all the children of God, who also say, "Here I am." In His presence, it is not "I", but "we" who are connected to Jesus. As St. Augustine says, "We pray to Him, through Him, in Him and we speak along with Him and He along with us." My union with Jesus and with others enables me to pray for one another.

Meditation:

After the preparatory steps:

I am having the meeting point within me because of Christ's Presence in me. Let me think of one of many that have asked for my prayers right now. *Lord Jesus, I bring before you this one (name) you knew before I ask what is his (her) needs. Lord bless him. May my prayer rise before you. I shall sing with the Psalmist:*

> *Lord, hear my prayer;*
> *In your faithfulness listen to my pleading;*
> *answer me in your justice (143:1).*

Notes:

Chapter 38
Basil Pennington, *the Eucharist yesterday and today*, (NY: Crossroad, 1984), p.2.

Chapter 39
1. Albert Nolan, *Jesus today,* (NJ: Orbis books, 2006), p.143.
2. Fulton J. Sheen, *These are the sacraments*, (NY: Hawthorn, 1962), p.49.
3. St John Chrysostom's quote from Mike Aquilina, *Fire of God's love; 120 reflections on the Eucharist,* (OH: Servant books, 2009), p.33.

Chapter 40
1. Sisters of Charity, *All creations sing, Praying the Psalms with Elizabeth Seton* (Bronx: Sisters of charity, 2009), p.30.
2. Timothy M.Dolan, *Priests for the Third millennium*, (Our Sunday Visitor, Inc.2000), p.204.
3. Ref: www.earlychristianwritings.com.Church fathers
4. Quote from First apology, from Ralph Wright, OSB, *Our Daily bread*, (NY/Mahwah, Paulist Press, 2008), p.13.
5. St. Ignatius quote from, Owen Cummings, *Eucharistic doctors,* (NY/Mahwah: Paulist Press, 2005), p.10.
6. St Cyprian's quote from Ralph Wright, OSB, *Our Daily Bread,* (NY/Mahwah: Paulist press, page17
7. Ibid., p.25.
8. Bendedict Groeschel., *Praying in the presence of our Lord*, (Our Sunday visitor, inc.Indiana 1999) p.64

Chapter 41
1. Thomas Merton, *The inner Experience*, (HarperSanfrancisco.2003), p.22
2. St. Augustine's quote from Ralph Wright, OSB, *Our Daily Bread*, (NY/Mahwah: Paulist Press, 2008), p. 27.
3. PopeBenedict XVI, *The Eucharist-Spiritual Thoughts series,* (USCCB, 2009) p.20
4. Ibid., p. 20.
5. Ibid., p.30.

Chapter 42
1. Thomas Keating, *The Heart of the World*, (The crossword Publishing co.; 1999), p.65
2. Pope Benedict XVI, *The Eucharist*-Spiritual Thoughts Series, (USCCB, 2009), page19

3. Thomas Keating, *The Heart of the World*, (NY: The crossword Publishing Co.; 1999), p.64.

4. St. John Vianney's quote from Mike Aquilina, *Fire of God's love,120 reflections on the Eucharist,* (OH: Servant Books, 2009), p. 63

IX. My Witness

43. I Am Touched by God's Power of Forgiveness.

As far as Jesus was concerned, whatever
measure of guilt anyone might have is a
matter for forgiveness, not condemnation.

Albert Nolan[1]

*At one of the retreats for the college professors of
Women's College, the participants included women religious and
ladies. On the final day of the three day retreat, I was asked to
prepare them for the Sacrament of Reconciliation. In order to
give an experience of the fascinating power of God's forgiveness,
I brought in the topic:* **Where there is perfect understanding,
there is no condemnation.**

*As the participants were women, I brought in a practical
example of mother's love for the child. Here is what I said:*

*Imagine you have a two-year-old child. In our culture, as
the evening draws, most of you have the responsibility to give a
simple wash to the child, and change the dress the child has with
a new one. Thereafter, imagine the child asks your permission to
go to the backyard to play with the neighbor's children. And you
say to your child, "Honey, just now I washed you and changed
your dress. Keep your clothes clean; don't get them dirty." The
child plays with the other children, and falls into the mud. Now
the child comes back with all the clothes dirty with the mud. What
will be your reaction? How many would give a simple smack to*

the child? Some of the mothers smilingly raised their hands to approve a little smacking. Imagine you smack the child...Is it not the projection of your problem? Most agree the problem was with them and not with the child. The problem is that mothers have lots of responsibility at home. Each one requires some time, and so the mother goes from one thing to another. If they have to go back to the same work once again, the mother may lose her cool and take it out on the child. This is something that is a natural consequence.

Now comes another interesting possibility. The child goes out to the backyard, and you see another child pushing your child into the mud, and now your child is returning to you. Will you smack this time? All of them said, "No!" Why? It is because you have an understanding of what happened. When you understand, you don't condemn.

The All Perfect God has a perfect understanding of how and why people sin. As sinners, we don't understand why we sin. We have the quilty predicament of what St Paul says of us: "What I do, I do not understand. For I do not do what I want. But I do what I hate" (Rom 7:15). Only God knows why we sin. And so where there is the perfect understanding, there cannot be condemnation. And so God only forgives.

Forgiveness is the most consoling gift of God but a complex one to comprehend. There have been a number of debates about forgiveness, whether or not it is conditional or unconditional. *Conditional* refers to forgiveness granted to a sinner only if he fulfills what is required: "Forgive and you will be forgiven" (Lk 5:37b). *Unconditional* does not depend upon the sinner's requirements: "Love your enemies, pray for those who persecute you" (Mt 5:44). Let us admit both the arguments are convincing to us. In the context of this chapter, we need to go beyond these arguments to see this gift of forgiveness from the mystical experience of human thirst and Divine love.

In the OT, there was this tension on the part of the people to understand 'God of mercy' and 'God of justice.' On the one hand, one thanks God for His mercy, and on the other, he is afraid of His justice. There are numerous occasions where people have expressed it. For example, "The LORD is slow to anger and rich in kindness, forgiving wickedness and crime; yet declaring the guiltless guilty, but punishing children and grandchildren to the third and fourth generation for their fathers' wickedness!"(Nm 14:17. cf. also Ex 34:6, 7). Another example, "A jealous and avenging God is the Lord, and avenger is the LORD, and angry; The Lord brings vengeance on his adversaries, lays up wrath for his enemies. The Lord is slow to anger, yet great in power, and the Lord never leaves the guilty unpunished" (Na 1:30). The simple word "yet" in both examples makes it complex to understand the message. Actually "yet" denotes to us the tension people had about the forgiveness and the justice. God does not have tension. It is the human understanding which has the tension. The tension is about praising God for his kindness to forgive them and dealing with the fear of punishment. The ideas of *vengeful* God, *jealous* God, *punishing* God, as we have seen in the chapter, are expressions of the crude understanding of human mind, that is, anthropomorphism.

The Book of Psalms has the typical prayers for forgiveness where we notice the same tension. For example, the popular Psalm 51 prays, "Have mercy on me, God in your goodness; in your abundant compassion blot out my offense" (v.1). And yet we read, "Do not drive me from your presence, take from me your Holy Spirit" (v.13). These are typical expressions of the tension. People even prayed to God pleading not to act out of anger. For example, Ps 85, "Will you be angry with us forever, drag out your anger for all generations?" (v.6). Another example, Ps 89, "How long, O Lord? Will you hide yourself forever? Will your wrath burn like fire?" (v.47). This is the typical scare of the OT people.

NT changed this 'tension- scenario' a little bit. The mindset of the people was such that Jesus had to talk to them in parables about forgiveness, and do miracles associated with the forgiveness. When Jesus said, *your sins are forgiven* (Mt 9:2), the person concerned knew Jesus has the perfect understanding of their context and their sins. Also, when Jesus condemned the sin to say: *Go and sin no more* (Jn 8:11b), the person concerned knew Jesus has the perfect understanding of their sin. His teaching about forgiveness and dealing with sinners would ultimately reach its powerful manifestation on the cross. "Father, forgive them, they know not what they do" (Lk 23: 34). This is the beautiful expression of where there is perfect understanding, there is no condemnation.

Eucharist is the new and everlasting covenant. According to the new covenant established by Jesus, every priest consecrates the wine to the effect of shedding for all so that sins may be forgiven. St. Paul's assurance, "In him we have redemption by his blood, the forgiveness of transgressions, in accord with the riches of his grace that he lavished upon us" (Eph 1:7,8) adds to the experience of God's forgiveness at every Eucharistic celebration. Jesus in the Eucharist forgives the sins of all. Anyone who is drawn to the Eucharist experiences His grace of forgiveness.

My Personal Context:

The sins are before me. I may not understand why I sinned. People may not understand me. Instead of looking at my sins, let me focus on the Presence of Jesus in the Eucharist. The Lord in the Eucharist tells me, 'I understand you. I shall never condemn you.' I consider this as the everlasting invitation for me to taste the power of His forgiveness.

Meditation:

After the preparatory steps:

Jesus is within me. He understands me, why I sinned. He only forgives me .He never condemns me. As I remember all my sins, Jesus is assuring me of His understanding to forgive me. Let me pray to Jesus: *Lord Jesus, I thank you for your forgiving presence in me. Let me have your grace within me always to be loyal to you to sin no more? Let me pray with the Psalmist:*

The Lord redeems loyal servants;

no one is condemned whose refuge is God(35:23).

44. I Forgive Others.

Those who love with the kind of love
asked for by Jesus are exposed to more
hatred and ridicule and persecution than
those who do not love that fully.

Bernard Lee[1]

"Can I talk to a priest?" A phone call was transferred to me in the rectory. The person wanted to remain anonymous. And so, let me call her Helen. After making sure that she was talking to a priest, she asked, "If I take away my life myself, will I end up in hell?" Embarrassed a bit, but realizing the sincerity of her anxiety in her way of asking, I asked, "Before I answer you, may I ask you if you could be comfortable to tell me what makes you ask a priest this question?" She said, "I am a Catholic. I am not a regular church goer, but I believe in God and I was taught always that those who commit suicide go to hell."

After getting a hint at her faith in prayer, I proceeded to ask, "Well, you seem to believe in prayer. Can I be of little assistance to you by praying for you to change your mind from ending your life?" There came the reply: "Oh yes! I believe in prayer. I have been praying a lot. It does not help me!" I asked, "Since you believe in prayer, why don't your come to church to pray?" She refused right away, "Oh no! I don't want to be a hypocrite. When I come to church I cannot pray. I only think of all those who have betrayed me, disowned me, abandoned me. I am angry with all. I pray at home. It is not of much help. Coming to church will not be of any help!"

In keeping with the anonymity of Helen's story, I can only say that it is all about experiencing abandonment by her family members, betrayal, asking to move out of the house, and feeling lonely. The usual ending, "I cannot take any more," was the tone of reason to end her life. Helen's story may not be unique.

Each of us goes through lots of difficulties such as these. It begins with each of us. We are not able to forgive our guilt, and so we are not able to forgive that of others. "Others" include brothers, sisters, family members, friends, people of other nationality, religion, class, status, etc. How do we forgive others? Is it possible to pray for them? It is possible provided each of us begins to experience God's forgiveness for our own sins. As we have seen in the previous chapter, God's forgiveness is there for us all the time. The power of forgiveness resides within us. It is with that power we forgive others. Forgiveness proceeds from the Power of God.

God's love reached its magnitude on the Cross of Jesus. Before embracing His Cross, Jesus prepared the minds of the people to carry the cross in their lives: "Whoever wishes to come after me must deny himself, take up his cross, and follow me" (Mk 8:34). The exemplary washing of the feet of others by Jesus at the Last Supper is an ultimate expression of self-denial. This example is meant for anyone who follows Jesus. It is always a challenge to live an authentic life. The authenticity begins with denying one's own self. One should be prepared to give up his or her own selfish ways of living. Self asserts itself always in comparison to others. It is in comparison with others that self has to make up his mind to be rude or to be kind, to be demanding or to be forgiving. When it comes to forgiveness one has to deny himself, and be prepared to forgive others their offenses.

Forgiveness is neither a feeling nor an emotion. Feelings and emotions change according to the mood of the person. Forgiveness is the greatest form of denying oneself, and so it is a definite decision. This decision is like taking up the cross. This decision exposes one *to more hatred, and ridicule, and persecution.* That is, when we are willing to forgive the offender, the offender may take for granted the forgiveness and commit the offense again and again. That is why, after the example of washing of the feet, Jesus cautioned the disciples to be willing to face the world: the hatred and ridicule and persecution. Jesus said, "If the world hates you, remember that it hated me first. If you belonged to the world, the world would love its own; but because you do not belong to the world, and I have chosen you out of the world, the world hates you" (Jn 15:18, 19). Is it possible at all for someone to face such a humiliation? In the judgement of the world, we can conclude the reactions: "It is too much." "This is ridiculous."

Jesus was aware of this difficult way of life to forgive others and to be ridiculed by the same. Jesus was aware of His own persecution to tell us this: *"if they persecuted me, they will also persecute you."* Jesus had His persecution, and He was leaving the world. And so he prayed for the disciples, *"And now I will no longer be in the world, but they are in the world, while I am coming to you. Holy Father, keep them in your name that you have given me, so that they may be one just as we are."* This prayer is what bestowed upon the disciples the necessary grace to live up to their call, which includes the virtue of forgiving others. In as much as it is very difficult to forgive and to be ridiculed, it is also the indwelling grace that helps one to face the world. Just as Jesus and the Father are one, each of us is one with Jesus within us. So the decision to forgive others is given by the indwelling Presence of Jesus.

St. Paul looked at the challenge of forgiving others. He knew it is possible with the power of the indwelling Spirit of Christ. Yet he looked at the world out there that would try to convince us. And so, he cautioned us in his letter to the Colossians, "See to it that no one captivate you with an empty, seductive philosophy according to human tradition, according to the elemental power of the world and not according to Christ"

(2:8). The world can easily convince people that it is ridiculous to forgive others and to be insulted by them. That is why St. Paul gave the most practical advice: "Put on then as God's chosen ones, holy and beloved, heartfelt compassion, kindness, humility, gentleness, and patience, bearing with one another and forgiving one another, if one has grievance against another; as the Lord has forgiven you, so must you also do"(3:12).

Can we live up to the expectations of St. Paul? It is certainly possible with Christ dwelling in us. Eucharist is the means to enrich the indwelling grace. St. Thomas Aquinas experiencing the Power of the Eucharist puts it, "No sacrament contributes more to our salvation than this; for it purges away our sins, increases our virtues, and nourishes our minds with an abundance of all the spiritual gifts."[2] Thus we experience God's forgiveness of our own sins, which in turn makes us forgive those of others.

My Personal Context:

As God's beloved, I am aware of Jesus dwelling within me. The more I am in touch with His Presence in me, the more I am aware of His mercy for me. The more I am in touch with His mercy the more I am able to forgive the offenses of others. I am also aware of the predicament of those people who don't forgive their own offenses are the people who are prone not to forgive others. So the more I realize God forgives me, the more I realize I am an instrument of forgiveness.

Meditation:

After the preparatory steps:

Jesus forgives me. That is why He is within me. With His presence within me, I shall forgive the sins of others. Experiencing God's forgiveness for me and forgiving others makes me worthy to pray the Lords Prayer, and to pray, " forgive our trespasses as we forgive those who trespass against us." Let me pray, "*O Lord Jesus. It is your mercy for me that increases within me the grace of forgiving others. Let me pray for this person (...) Let your forgiveness reach out to him (her),and let me live happily even if the person hates me. Let me praise you with the Psalmist:*

> *Bless the Lord, my soul;*
> *do not forget all the gifts of God*
> *Who pardons all your sins,*
> *heals all your ills (103:2,3).*

45. I Consecrate Myself in Truth

To be made holy in truth means to accept
truth as the revelation of God not in any
abstract sense but in the fullest meaning of
God entering into human life.

John F O'Grady[1]

Sr. Mary Linda is one of the Sacramentine Sisters. Her story is fascinating in so far as the Eucharistic experience is concerned. She joined the Sisters of Charity Federation, Carrolton, Ohio. The main ministry of the Sisters is to teach. Though she was happy with this for about 9 years, her service took a different direction: to be a contemplative nun. It was because she had an interest in the Real Presence of the Lord in the Eucharist.

Asked what she had to say about her move from an "active" religious to a "contemplative" religious, Sister responded: "As a child I was drawn to the Eucharist." She began to reminisce about her father who would take her close to the altar rail. He would point out Jesus, and ask her to talk to Jesus. As a child, she was happy to talk to Jesus in the Eucharist.

About the transition from 'active' to the 'contemplative' life, she recalled that it all began on a Sunday. She had to supervise the girls in the pool. Something prompted within her: "What could I do that would connect me to all the people instead

289

of few girls? She listened to an inner voice that prompted her to pick up a copy of the Catholic Digest. There she read a vocation guide to the Cloistered Sacramentine sisters and their life of prayer in the Presence of the Blessed Sacrament. She joined them, and she has passed 29 years praying in front of the Blessed Sacrament. "It is wonderful to be consecrated to the Lord in the Eucharist. Taking time with the Lord for those who do not have time is my fulfillment," she said.

To be consecrated to the Lord is not only a privilege to the nuns and priests, but to all who are connected to the Eucharist. It is a mystical but practical way of life. When Jesus prayed at the Last Supper for his disciples for their consecration in truth, He added, "I pray not only for them, but also for those who will believe in me through their word." It is evident from the Lord's Prayer that all the worshipers of the Eucharist can enjoy the consecration in truth.

What is truth? This has perplexed the minds of many in the course of history. Standing at the trial before Pilate, Jesus said, "For this I was born and for this I came into the world, to testify to the truth. Everyone who belongs to the truth listens to my voice." Pilate did not know what Jesus was talking about. The fact about Jesus testifying to the truth did not make any sense to Pilate. That is why Pilate expressed his own ignorance, "What is truth?"

The word Truth is the translation of the Hebrew word *emet,* which means something that is firm and solid. It is so secure and strong that one can trust without any doubt. In the Old Testament understanding, God alone is truthful and so people trusted in God alone. The prophet Isaiah would say to the people, "Trust in the Lord for ever! For the Lord is eternal Rock" (Is 26:4). Truth is ultimately this: God alone can be trusted.

Emet is opposed to falsehood People would compare what is trustworthy with what is false. That is why people would say, "Better to take refuge in the Lord than to put one's trust in mortals" (Ps 118:8; cf. also Ps 62:8, 56:5). The Book of Wisdom says, "Those who trust in him shall understand truth, and the faithful shall abide with him in love: Because grace and mercy are with his holy ones, and his care is with his elect" (Wis. 3:9). What is unfolding here is that Grace is associated with Truth. God alone can bestow upon us the grace and mercy, which would be taken up by St. John in the New Testament.

St. John writing his Gospel introduces Jesus as the Word becoming flesh to dwell with us. He continues to unfold the glory of Jesus as grace and truth: "We saw his glory, the glory as of the Father's only Son, full of grace and truth" (Jn 1:14b). The Prologue of the Gospel of St. John shows that John's readers were already familiar with the Greek term *aletheia* for truth. Aletheia is a dynamic word. Its root 'slm' denotes something that is 'not hidden' but becomes the basis for something evident. So aletheia means something that is a basic principle or power or reality behind the appearance of a person or a thing, without which that person or that thing cannot exist.

Aletheia as applied to Jesus means Jesus' abiding Presence in a person is a reality or a principle or a power that gives life to the person. We should remember St. John was a mystic compared to any other Gospel writer. His mystical understanding is so evident in proclaiming Jesus the Truth. John recorded Jesus' startling statement about the mystical union between him and us: "Whoever remains in me and I in him will bear much fruit, because without me you can do nothing" (Jn 15:5b). For St. John, Jesus is the Truth. He alone can abide within us. The effect of Jesus' Presence cannot be hidden as His presence is what gives grace to all in whom He abides.

At the Last Supper, Jesus prayed for his disciples. The prayer- "Consecrate *them in the Truth. Your word is truth. As you sent me into the world, so I send them into the world. And I consecrate myself for them, so that they may be consecrated in truth"*- is one of the amazing prayers. It is amazing because it conveys to anyone the life and mission of Jesus that John wanted to tell his listeners. Jesus, the Word (Jn 1:1), became flesh to dwell within us (Jn 1:14). He is the source of grace and truth (Jn 1:14b). And so, only Jesus, the Truth sets us free (Jn 8:32). He alone is Truth, the Way and the Life (Jn 14:6). Jesus alone can fill us with his abiding Presence (Jn 17:21). It is for the world's salvation (Jn 17:23). Thus we see the mission accomplishment in Jesus' prayer.

Eucharist is His abiding Presence with us. When we receive the Eucharist, His abiding Presence unites us with Him. This is the consecration we experience within us. Jesus becomes the truth not hidden, but so evident to give us the grace to be united with Him. This is the experience- *"because of the truth that dwells in us and will be with us forever (1Jn 1:2)-* that made St John bless the first Christians: " Grace, mercy, and peace will be with us from God the Father and from Jesus Christ the Father's Son in truth and love" (1Jn 1:3).

My Personal Context:

When I worship Jesus in the Eucharist, Jesus' words to the Samaritan woman are accomplished in me. I remind myself of those words of Jesus: "But the hour is coming, and is now here, when true worshipers will worship the father in Spirit and truth, and indeed the Father seeks such people to worship him"(Jn 4:23). I realize I am one of "such people." It is a privilege to be counted among such people to worship Jesus in the Eucharist.

Meditation:

After the preparatory steps:

Jesus in me is the Truth because He abides in me. His abiding Presence is His Spirit. The Spirit directs me to worship the true living God. It is in and through this worship I am being set free here on earth and in heaven. Let me pray: *Lord Jesus, it is an amazing experience to realize that you are abiding within me. Let me praise you that you are the Truth! Let your truthful Presence in me continue to save me and others in the world. I shall be conscious of my inmost being so as to preserve Your Presence within me along with the Psalmist:*

> *Still, you insist on sincerity of heart*
> *In my inmost being teach me wisdom (51:8).*

46. I Love My Priests

The primary association of the priesthood,
both in the consciousness of the Christian people
and in the self-understanding of the priest himself,
is with the Eucharist.

Cardinal Sean O'Malley[1]

Michael and Wendi, one of the faithful couples are devoted to the Eucharist. They have on their car a bumper sticker: **We love our priests**. *When Michael was asked about it, he said that he happened to be part of the celebration called youth for 2000 in Long Island. There he came across this sticker. "I loved it," he said, "We have priests who are specially chosen for our sake. They give us the Eucharist. They give us God's blessings. We thought we should be grateful to our priests. With all the scandals the media were projecting about our priests, we wanted to be counter-cultural. So we decided to have this bumper sticker." I was happy to thank him for displaying the sticker. As a daily communicant, he realizes the worth of any priest in the Church.*

Dr. Ernie and his wife Bunny are Eucharistic ministers. Ernie is also a lector. At the end of every Mass he participates in, he would always go over to the priest to say, "Thank you for celebrating the Mass for us." When asked about this grateful gesture, he said, "We cannot take our priests for granted.

Without you we cannot have the Eucharist. Elsewhere people don't have the daily Eucharist due to the shortage of priests. I think we should be grateful to you."

Michael and Wendi, Ernie and Bunny realize that they have to be grateful for the priests. I remember, at one of the priests' retreat, I started the spiritual talk on the Eucharist this way: **No priest, no Eucharist! No Eucharist, no Church! No Church, no redemption!** *Simply put, the salvation of the world depends on the priests. It may sound an exaggerated conclusion, but it is the reality. Probably it is this reality that makes these grateful couples and thousands of others in the world to be grateful to the priests.*

Priesthood is first and foremost a gift to the people. It is not so much a personal gift for the one who is called but a gift for all the people. Every priest is a gift from God to the community of people. The gift of priesthood is cherished and shared by the community of the people because of their own 'common priesthood.' If there is no common priesthood, there is no ministerial priesthood. It is in Christ everyone is connected to the royal priesthood (cf. 1Pet 2:9).

St. John attributes the power of the Blood of Jesus that connects all of us. He puts it, "To him who loves us and has freed us from our sins by his blood, who has made into a kingdom, priests for his God and Father...." (Rev 1:5b, 6). His

Blood that freed us from sins, continues to free us with His Presence in and through the Eucharist. So it is the Eucharistic Presence that frees us all and connects us all into a common priesthood. As Fr. Lawrence Freeman puts it, "The essential dynamic of Christian priesthood is always one of ministry, above all Eucharistic ministry, to the people of God who themselves share in the priesthood of Christ." There is no other way the Eucharistic Presence is there in the world without the priests. That is why the priesthood is the gift to the people who cannot be connected to one another without this gift.

Another grateful way of looking at this gift to the people is the fact that priests are taken from among the people. As it is said in the Letter to the Hebrews, "Every high priest is taken from among men and made their representative before God, to offer gifts and sacrifices for sins" (Heb 5:1). A priest is not specially created a priest. He is chosen form among men. And so, he becomes a gift to the people.

Another profound way of looking at this gift is from the everlasting gift of the Eucharist. The primary gift that the priest gives to the people is the Eucharist. It is by the Eucharist that He gives life to the world. He said, "…the bread I give is my flesh for the life of the world" (Jn 6:51b). Life of the world! What does the "life" entail? Jesus is not just meant for the people of His time. He is the Savior of the world. It is the Eucharistic

Presence that goes beyond time and place to be available to give life. There is not a single country in the world where the Eucharist is not celebrated. Even if we come up with one, let us remember the Power of the Eucharist can reach all the ends of the earth as it was foretold by Isaiah of Jesus: "All the ends of the earth will behold the salvation of our God"(Is 52:10b).

Jesus' Presence reaches everyone in the world. As *Ecclesia de Eucharista* of Pope John Paul II puts it, "Eucharist embraces all creation. The Son of God became man in order to restore all creation, in one supreme act of praise, to the one who made it from nothing."[2] It is the Eucharist that has the power to reach every human being from all the ends of the world. So we can say that all the ends of the earth has seen the salvation in Christ who is in the Eucharist. The priesthood is truly a profound gift for the life of the world.

Another way of looking at this gift is to look at Jesus, who has taken priests as gift to Himself. At the institution of the Eucharist and the priesthood at the Last Supper, Jesus is praying for his disciples. This prayer is known in the church as priestly prayer. Jesus concluded his prayer, profoundly acknowledging that priests are a gift to him. "Father, they are your gift to me. I wish where I am they also may be with me, that they may see my glory that you gave me, because you loved me before the foundation of the world" (Jn 17:24). The mystical meaning of this prayer helps us realize that priests are united with Jesus in the Eucharist.

Priests have the responsibility, which I term 'mystical responsibility.' Priests have mystical union with Jesus when they say the words of consecration. Each priest is another Christ- *where I am they may be with me-* is realized as they say those words. They take up the command: "Do this in memory of me" as the result of this personal but mystical responsibility. Thanks to each priest who has become a gift to Christ, we have the Eucharist.

Whenever we hear the scandals related to the priests, we only have to go back to the Last Supper story. In spite of the betrayal of Judas and the denial of Peter, the power of the priesthood and the Eucharist continues to this day. The mystical union with Jesus and the mystical responsibility is the key, and this awareness will put an end to the scandals. The "betrayals" and the "denials" cannot undo the power of the Eucharist. Eucharist will remain forever until we continue the eternal banquet as it is revealed in the Book of Revelation: "Blessed are those who have been called to the wedding feast of the Lamb" (Rev 19:9).

My Personal Context:

My priests are a gift to me from God. I will gladly identify myself with the Testament of St. Francis of Assisi: *"I refuse to consider their sins, because I can see the Son of God in them and they are better than I. I do this because in this world I cannot see the most high Son of God with my own eyes, except for his most holy Body and Blood which they receive and administer to others.*[3]

Mediation:

After the preparatory steps:

I have Jesus within me, thanks to my priests who said the words of consecration. I am grateful to the priests. Let me now be connected with my priests in my prayer: *Lord Jesus, You are the eternal priest. Your presence in priests has made them an awesome gift to me. Let me be grateful to them till the end of life as I am going to share with the eternal banquet. I shall join the Palmist to thank you for my priest:*

> *Blessed is he who comes in the name of the LORD.*
> *We bless you from the LORD's house (118:26).*

47. I Live by the Unconditional Love of God

Christ's body and blood, the laying down
of his own life for love of human life and
for his friends, reveals to us the depths of
God's love and so brings salvation to the
whole world.
Anthony Campbell[1]

*There was an interesting story connected with Admiral
Ronald L. Pereira of India. He was the Chief of the Indian Navy
from 1979 to 1982. In India, this was one of few prestigious
Government positions served by a Catholic at that time. A few
years after his retirement, he chose to live in a place called
Wellington Barracks, which is in South India. This area comes
under the Ootacamund Diocese, India. I happened to be the
Parish priest during that time. He was daily communicant, and
he was known for his practicing faith.*

*One time he was admitted to the hospital. He asked me if
he could make his confession in the hospital and receive
Communion. On one such hospital visit to him, he managed to
get up from his bed, held my hand and said, "Father, can I ask
you one thing?" "Sure," I said. He asked, "Father, will I get to
heaven?" "Of course," I said, "You will get to heaven." He
asked, "How come you are so sure?" I said, "It is because God
is love, and God loves you." Then the conversation was switched
to the love of God, and to the remarkable book, The*

301

Unconditional Love of God by Fr. John Powell, S.J. He asked if he could borrow the book. He was fascinated to read all the compelling proofs of God's unconditional love. During my next visit to him, he said, "Why don't you priests talk about this gift of God's unconditional love. Mostly I hear from the pulpit the fire and brimstone God?"

God's love is totally unconditional. 'Unconditional' means God's love is not merited by us by doing something to deserve it. It is freely given to us. It was revealed to us in Jesus Christ. It took so many thousands of years to accept it. Why? Probably it is due to the human experience of conditional love.

Human experience reveals that human love is limited because it is conditional. Let it be between husband and wife, or parents and children, or among friends, human experience has love as conditional. Even the strongest love seems to hinge upon conditions. For example, when a husband says, "I cannot think of my life without her," it's a typical appreciation for the conditions that are being fulfilled. Every broken love-relationship is about the conditions that were not respected by one of them. The best example for unconditional love is the love of a mother for her child. Yet, when the child grows up, conditions are in place, and so we hear about the rejection of love between the mother and child. This human experience is what is behind the difficulty of understanding the unconditional love of God for us. Yet psychology reveals that every human being has an innate desire for the unconditional love.

God alone can fulfill the longing in humans for the unconditional love. Yet the conditional mind of humans never comprehended this from the beginning. They responded to God's love with the 'conditional mind.' of human experience. For example, when God said to Moses, "You are my intimate friend." and also, "You have found favor with me," Moses could not comprehend it. He said, "If I have found favor with you, do let me know your ways so that, in knowing you, I may continue to find favor with you." When you analyze Moses' response, his conditional mind comes up with the word, "If." There cannot be 'if' and 'when' and 'because' in the unconditional love of God. The 'if' of Moses was the projection of his 'conditional' mind to ask the Lord for the ways to fulfill so as to continue to have God's favor. This has been part of our human culture by which we try to fulfill something in order to merit God's love.

The other consequence of the 'conditional mind' is the confusion about God's love and justice. For example, Abraham was confused about God's way of punishment that makes the innocent die with the guilty (Gen 18:25). He even asked God: "Should not the Judge of all the world act with justice?" Why should Abraham remind God to behave justly? It does not make sense. This is definitely one of the anthropomorphisms, as seen in previous chapters. This is again the case of the projection of human mind that could not grasp the depth of God's love.

These experiences had left such an impact on human beings, that they were obsessed with legalities to merit the love of God. The obsessions included, to 'pray' to merit the blessings, to 'do penance' to merit the forgiveness. The radical change came into effect with the coming of Jesus: "The Sabbath was made for man and not man for the Sabbath" (Mk 2:27). This was the turning point for the people of Jesus' time. In God's ways, man is more important than the law.

In Jesus, people saw God who loved the world that He gave His only Son (cf. Jn 3:16). Jesus proclaimed that God "makes his sun rise on the bad and the good, and causes rain to fall on the just and the unjust" (Mt 5:45). He revealed His Father's nature to give the same wages to "the first and the last" (Mt 20: 16). He had no hesitation to say, "I did not come to call the righteous but sinners" (Mt 9:13). He announced His Father's love and mercy that does not care about 'the penance' of the prodigal son but to throw the party for him (cf. Lk 15). John, the beloved Apostle, realized all this, and so he proclaimed the greatest truth which the world had long waited to hear. That is: *God is love, and whoever remains in love remains in God and God in him (1Jn 4:16).* By proclaiming, "We love because God loved us first"(1Jn 4:9), John wants us to accept that God's love is behind every love relationship. And by proclaiming, "There is no fear in perfect love," John wants us to understand that the love is unconditional. Each human being can now celebrate God's love without any sense of fear.

The Greek word for Love is *eros, philia* and *agape*. *Eros* is more connected with romantic feeling, and the *philia* was with friendship. Agape is something unique because it is totally selfless and does not change. Though the sacred writers used eros and philia, they used agape more frequently. It is because agape brings out the unconditional nature of love. Pope Benedict XVI in his first encyclical, *Deus caritas est,* teaches us the unconditional nature of God's love: "God's eros for man is also totally agape. This is not only because it is bestowed in a completely gratuitous manner without any previous merit, but also because it is love which forgives" (10). This tells us so succinctly of Gods unconditional love.

Eucharist is the Presence of God's unconditional love. Jesus made it according to the New Covenant. "New," because it is totally unconditional unlike the Old one which was conditional. The New Covenant love is totally experienced, as Jesus asking the Father, after the institution of the Eucharist, "that love with which you loved me may be in them and I in them" (Jn 17:26).And so the abiding Presence is the experience of unconditional love of God.

My Personal Context:

I realize that 'prayers,' 'penance,' 'commandments' are not 'conditions' but the deepest gratitude I owe to God and others for His unconditional love. The more I understand the depth of God's love, the more I am faithful to pray. The more I experience the forgiving love, the more I forgive others. The more I grasp the unconditional love, the more I walk extra miles for others. As John Powell puts it, "Love is more demanding than law."[2]

Meditation:

After the preparatory steps:

Jesus is within me not because I deserve Him to be within me. It is because of His unconditional love. Let me pray: *Lord, Make me an instrument of unconditional love in all I say and do. I shall join the psalmist to sing your praises:*

> *The lord's love for us is strong*
> *The Lord is faithful forever (117:2).*

Notes:

Chapter 43

1. Albert Nolan, *Jesus Today*, (Mary knoll, NY: Orbis books, 2007), p.86

Chapter 44

1. Bernard Lee, *Becoming of the church*, (Paulist Press, NY: Paramus, Toronto, 1974), p. 185

2. Ref. from Ralph Wright, *Our Daily Bread*, (NY/Mahwah, NJ: Paulist Press, 2008), p. 69

Chapter 45

1. John F.O'Grady, *According to John*. (NY/Mahwah, NJ: Paulist Press, 1999), p. 90.

Chapter 46.

1. Cardianl Sean O' Mally, Preface for *The Priest hood*, by Pope Benedict XVI, (Washington D.C.: USCCB Publishing, 2009).

2. Pope John Paul II, Encyclical on Ecclesia de Eucharistia, 2003, #38.

3. Francis of Assisi quotes from www. Fordham.edu/halsall/source,stfran.html.

Chapter 47

1. Anthony F. Campbell, S.J, *God first loved us*, (Mahwah, NJ: Paulist press, 2000), p. 69.

2. John Powell, *A life giving vision*, (Thomas More Publishing, 1995), p. 268

X. My Glory

48. I Sing God's Praises

Music probably began as a religious act to
accompany ritual. It continues to play a
vital role in the life of faith.
Within worship, it sustains us when a
service grows dull,
and teaches profound truths enjoyably.

Kathy Coffey[1]

*Tom is one of the choir members and a cantor for almost
twenty-three years. He is known for his active participation at the
liturgy. I asked him, "Tom, having a Masters Degree in the
Sacred Liturgy, it does not come a surprise that you are for
singing that is one of the ways of active participation. How do
you see your role as a cantor and a choir member in active
participation?" He reminisced about his early part of life, that he
would find easy to memorize anything in music form. When he
was introduced to "Jesus Christ, Superstar," he was deeply
touched by the part of the music connected with the scene of Mt.
of Olives in Luke 19:40. Jesus was acclaimed, " Blessed is the
King who comes in the name of the Lord..." The Pharisees told
Jesus to stop them from singing, and Jesus replied, "I tell you, if
they keep quiet, the stones will cry out!"*

*Tom relates Jesus remarks to the active participation. He
said, "Everyone should be self assured, It is okay for me to sing
even if mine is an ordinary voice; each one should find their own*

311

voice, and participate in singing. If we keep quiet, the 'stones' will cry out to sing." Tom had concluded, "If I don't sing, the stones will sing! Now with the Eucharist where His body and Blood has become part of me, there is no way it can keep me from singing His praises."

Theresa, the organist and music director at St. Mary's, Wappingers Falls, has her maxim for music: "Music is divine. Church music is not for show. It is only to praise God." The convictions of Tom and the dictum of Theresa express the profound and sacred nature of singing.

It is the profound human expression of acknowledging God's Presence. Singing is not an invention of the mind. It is a product of the heart. It is because humans can experience their interiority, which enjoys the beauty of the creation. Ultimately, God is the author and originator of music, as He created man's interiority after his own image and likeness.

Man is enjoying God's creation with his interority and singing God's praise. It goes back to the very story of creation. The Book of Genesis has the very first reference to music in the person of Jubal, who is from the lineage of Cain. Jubel was the "ancestor of all who play the lyre and the pipe" (Gen 4:21). From this first reference in Genesis to its last reference of the victory song in the Book of Revelation (19:5-8), we have hundreds of references to the musical instruments, singing, melody, voice etc.

This speaks volumes about the sacredness of music and the creative nature of man to acknowledge the beauty of creation.

The Creator already acknowledged the Beauty of Creation. God's own mind in enjoying the beauty is written by the sacred author: "God saw how good it was" (Gen 1:10,12). The first realization of the mystical experience was the musical experience, where humans blossomed to hear the symphony of God's Presence with the creation. Then followed the mystical experience of humans joining the whole of creation to sing God's praises. No wonder that we have those mystical songs (cf. Dn 3:52-90, Ps 148) where the whole creation is summoned to sing the praises of God. The Prophet Isaiah saw the vision of angels, who are connected with the whole world singing in heaven: *Holy, holy, holy is the Lord of hosts...All the earth is filled with his glory (Is 6:1-3).*

The new wave of mystical music came with the Incarnation of the Son of God. These praises were both mystical and realistic in their expression. *Mystical,* because heaven and earth joined to sing the Incarnation of God. The angels are now singing, "Glory to God in the highest and on earth peace to those to whom his favor rests" (Lk 2:14). *Realistic*, because humans have seen their Savior with their own eyes, and so they burst into song. It is said that the Shepherds went to see Jesus, and they returned "glorifying and praising God for all they had heard and seen just as it had been told to them" (Lk 2:20).

After three years of life and mission, Jesus knew that He had to go to Jerusalem to suffer. It is there Jesus would eventually institute the Eucharist, and die and rise again to be with us forever. On his entry into Jerusalem, the people proclaimed Jesus as Messiah by singing, "Blessed is the King who comes in the name of the Lord. Peace in heaven and glory in the highest." This hymn is the verse from Ps.118: 26. It became almost the prelude to the Lord who was about to institute the Eucharist. This hymn not only testifies the continuation of the singing of the Psalms, but also the continuation of the singing in the present day liturgy. At every Eucharistic celebration, we sing, "Holy, Holy, Holy Lord! Thus we continue the mystical experience of the past into the present and to the future heavenly worship.

Eucharist is the real Presence of Jesus manifested in the form of bread and wine. It is in receiving the Eucharist, we continue to experience the innate desire to praise God for His Presence in us. It is in the Eucharistic celebration, we, the NT people, continue the OT experience of praising the creator. We too mystically hear the symphony of the creator not with all creation but specifically with the bread and wine. It is in the Eucharist, we experience our mystical connection with the heavenly liturgy as it is revealed in the Book of Revelation (Cf.4). Ultimately, singing, that is the original response to the presence of God in the creation, now remains our response to God's presence in the Eucharist. It will find its final rhythm in heavenly liturgy.

Our participation in the sacred liturgy is the human expression of our hearts longing to blend with the angelic choir. As the famous liturgy Professor Enrico Massa puts it, "...the liturgy celebrated on earth should be the reflection of the angelic liturgy, a true copy of it. This meant the need of having on earth the same hymns that were being sung in the heavenly temple."[2] Our singing is now joined with that of angels. That is why, that at the celebration of each Eucharist, the celebrant invites us to join *the choir of angels to sing "Holy, Holy, Holy."* That moment adds up to the mystical experience of life we have found in the Eucharist.

My Personal Context:

Eucharist gives me the highest form of mystical relationship with God. The Lord who comes into me connects me with the heavenly liturgy. Whenever I sing at the Eucharistic celebration, I realize my mystical nature being strengthened by it. I shall be attuned to the encouraging words of St. Paul that invite me to sing Psalms, hymns and spiritual songs with gratitude in our hearts to God (cf. Col 3:16, Eph 5:18). Eucharist is the highest form of gratitude, where I join with my *mystical heart* that connects me with everyone in the world to sing His praises.

Meditation:

After the preparatory steps:

Jesus is within me. This mystical Oneness now joins me with everyone and every creation. With all the creation I now join the angelic choir. *Let me pray: Lord God, you gave me my voice which is not just mine, but the part of your mystical oneness with you, your angels and others. Let me now join the Psalmist to invite all to sing:*

> *Come, let us sing joyfully to the LORD*
> *Cry out to the rock of our salvation*
> *Let us greet him with a song of praise*
> *Joyfully sing out our psalms (95:1,2).*

49. I Find my Inner Joy

Joy is the echo of God's life within us.

Abbot Marmion[1]

Jerry and Gwen, a couple known for their love for the Eucharist, are Eucharistic ministers. They are renowned for their generosity and hospitality. One time at dinner with them at their home, Gwen said to me, "Father Dhas, you bring up the idea of inner joy many times in your sermon and homilies. Most of us are familiar with the idea of joy, not so much with the Inner joy. Will you help us comprehend what the "inner' is?" While I agreed with them that the idea of "inner" is not so familiar with many in the church, I complimented them for their quest to understand the "inner."

When people seek more insights into the "inner," it is a sign they are sincere in seeking their inner joy. Jerry and Gwen are among millions of people who are "seeking" the inner joy that would make a difference in their day to day life. Why should people seek it?

Seeking is a natural approach of man as it is something very human. Seeking is done within man. It cannot be found outside of him/ her. Man does not have to go to places or persons to find joy. Seeking has to do with the realm of "within," that is, with heart and soul. In the Old Testament, it is said, "…You shall

317

seek the LORD, your God; and you shall indeed find him when you search after him with your whole heart and with your whole soul" (Deut 4:29). The seeking has to be done with the whole heart and the whole soul. This means the search has to be from within man. Then we have the Prophet Jeremiah's assurance: "When you look for me you will find me. Yes, when you seek me with all your heart, you will find me with you..." (Jer 29:14). This is how man realized that seeking has to do with the "inner."

Though the "inner" is very much in every human, it can never be defined. It is because of its mystical nature. It is so much part of man that he seeks to locate it within himself. Thus man identifies the "within" or the "inner" with his own heart. That is why the "heart" is almost a synonym for the "inner." The Book of Proverbs says, "My son, if your heart is wise, my own heart will also rejoice; and my inmost being will exult, when your lips speak what is right"(23:15,16). The Book of Psalms has many such examples: "You insist on sincerity of heart: in my inmost being teach me wisdom" (51:8). "You have given my heart more joy" (Ps 4:8b). Thus seeking is an inner and sincere longing.

What is joy? Joy is the translation of the Hebrew word Simcha (pronounced as Sim kah) which is connected to the service of the Lord. When we serve God, we should *serve with joy* for His abundant blessings. Man responds to God to serve

Him with joy for His blessings. That is the reason why in the Old Testament, we read passages like, "Shout joyfully to the Lord" (Ps 100:1), "Come before him with joyful song" (100:3), "You will show me the path to life, abounding joy in your presence" (16:11). St. Peter would refer to this Psalm (16:11) in his famous speech on the Pentecost Day (cf. Acts 2:28). It means Joy is an inmost expression of serving God. This can be experienced only from within. The external sign is a vibrant strength to be at His service. This is the experience of Joy.

Let us turn to the Greek word of Joy. It is *Chara* which means a calm, quiet, serene joy. In other words it is found in the inner realm of a person. It is often with a peaceful atmosphere that one can experience joy within. Also, what is interesting is that Chara is derived from *Charis* that means grace. Grace is the initiative of God, and so, it is divine. So the God-given grace is what gives joy, and so it is a Divine experience. The OT idea of Joy that was for the service of God is now being deepened in the Greek understanding as the inner grace that motivates one to do that service.

At the institution of the Eucharist, during the farewell discourse, Jesus gave His joy to His disciples. For Jesus, joy is more than the service of the Lord. First, Jesus referred to joy as His joy: "I have told you this so that my joy might be in you and your joy might be complete" (Jn 15:11). "My Joy" refers to His

319

inner joy of His Father's abiding Presence in Him. The joy of Jesus becomes the joy of the disciples. Jesus is abiding in them. His abiding Presence becomes the joy in them.

Second, the world cannot give this joy. In order to distinguish inner joy from the outer one, let us use the word "happiness." Happiness in our experience never lasts. In contrast to the temporary happiness, joy is complete. That is the reason why Jesus further says, "…no one will take away your joy from you" (Jn 16:22b). "I speak this in the world so that they may share my joy completely" (Jn 17:13). The quality of inner joy is strong and complete. Even if people with the inner joy were to grieve a while "their grief will become joy" (Jn 16:20b).

Third, the outcome of joy is rejoicing. Jesus said, "I will see you again and your hearts will rejoice" (Jn 16:22a). Mary's experience is the perfect example of rejoicing. The indwelling Presence of Jesus makes Mary joyful and that in turn makes Mary rejoice. "My soul proclaims the greatness of the Lord; my spirit rejoices in God my Savior" (Lk 1:46). The message of the Incarnation from the Angel Gabriel takes form in the womb of Mary. Rejoicing is an outward exuberance to be for others. Mary, who had the joy of Jesus' presence in her womb, went to rejoice with Elizabeth.

St. Paul would say, "Rejoice in the Lord always. I shall say it again: rejoice!"(Phil 4:4). St. Paul brings up this concept of joy and rejoicing again and again in his letters (cf. 2 Cor 13:11, 1Thes 5:16). Rejoicing for St. Paul is associated with service for one another. In all his letters, he would instruct the early Christians to serve one another. This reflects the OT idea of joy that was in the service of the Lord. When St. Paul wrote to the Corinthians about the tradition of the Institution of the Eucharist (1Cor 11:23-26), what follows is his exhortation to the early Christians to be at the service of one another (cf. Chapters 12, 13). Rejoicing is to help, to support, and to care for others in the world. The Eucharistic Presence never wants one to keep the joy just for him but motivates him to rejoice with others.

Mary's joy helps us understand the joy of the Eucharist. Mary had Jesus within her womb. We have Jesus within us. When we receive the Lord in the Eucharist, we are like Mary experiencing the joy to rejoice with others. Rejoicing is the mystical exuberance that connects one to think of others always. "Receiving" the Eucharist is a way of seeking. Abiding Presence in us is the inner experience. Eucharistic Presence in us is what completes the joy. "…Your joy will be complete" (Jn 16:24b) refers not only to the permanent joy of the Eucharist that Jesus gives us, but also to the completion in heaven. As Pope John Paul II said, "Eucharist is a straining towards the goal, a foretaste of the fullness of joy promised by Christ (cf. Jn 15:11). It is in some way the anticipation of heaven, the pledge of future glory."[2] Nothing in the world can complete the joy but the Eucharist.

My Personal Context:

My inner self is my inner abode for Jesus. I recall St. Ephrem, a Fourth century saint. I am awakened to his prayer: "In Your sacrament we daily embrace You and receive You into our hearts; we have had Your treasure hidden within us ever since we received baptismal grace; it grows ever richer at Your sacramental table. Teach us to find joy in your favor."[3] This prayer mystically connects me with the saint's inner joy.

Meditation:

After the preparatory steps:

My inner most self is now the abode for Jesus to abide in me. Jesus is within me, giving me the joy that the world cannot give. I have the joy to rejoice in the Lord. Let me share this by rejoicing with others. Let me pray: *Lord Jesus, You are amazing with your Presence within me. Let me thank you for your joyous Presence that wells up joy within me. Let me join the Psalmist to affirm Your joy within me:*

> *Therefore my heart is glad, my soul rejoices;*
> *My body also dwells secure (16:9).*

322

50. I Die in Order to Rise with Him

Now, heaven has been unveiled for us with
the death and resurrection of Jesus Christ.
Now is the Communion God has created
us for. *Now* heaven touches earth and
awaits you.

Scott Hahn[1]

Jeanne is Eucharistic minister who has a profound devotion to the Eucharist. Jeanne called the rectory with the request if I could go up to the hospital to anoint Vincent, her brother-in- law. While proceeding to the hospital with Jeanne and her husband Ron in their car, I reminisced about her mom, Winnie who passed away a year back. Knowing Jeanne's faith, I asked, "Do you talk to your mom?" "Yes I did this morning, Father", was her immediate reply, "I asked for her prayers for Vincent and I told her that we are going to the hospital." This response of Jeanne reflected her childlike faith in her mom's resurrected life.

After administering the anointing of the sick to Vincent, Jeanne and I were returning in her car to the rectory. The conversation continued again about her mom. She has an absolute faith to see her mom in heaven. She considered it a privilege and blessing to have cared for her mom before her passing to be with God. She said, "Ron and I were privileged to have mom at home during her last few months. We took care of her. I would get up every morning saying, "What can I do today something more for my mom?" What an extraordinary thirst to serve ones parents in their advanced age?" Jeanne and Ron known as "simple and polite people" by the parishioners did not surprise me about their tremendous faith in the resurrected life. The Death and Resurrection of Our Lord is what gives our life meaning and purpose. Jeanne and Ron are the people whose outstanding faith explains the fundamental mystical reality of our Christian life, which culminate in our resurrected life.

In the OT, Moses' presence to the Presence of God is described this way: "The Lord used to speak to Moses face to face, as one man speaks to another" (Ex 33:11). *"Face to face"* should not be taken literally as it is said in the same chapter of Exodus, "But my face you cannot see, for no man sees me and still lives" (Ex 33:20). The author is using one of the forms of anthropomorphism, that is, to explain God-experience in a human way of speech. It is to express the reality of the mutual presence between God and man. And so, it could be understood as an experience of God's Presence. The fact of the matter is that every human has this longing to have God's Presence.

The Psalms testify to the fact that longing to see the face of God was very much part of human prayer. For example, "Come," says my heart, "seek God's face"; your face, LORD, do I seek!" (Ps 27: 8). The Psalmist has a longing that originates from within to see God face to face. Another example, "My being thirsts for God, the living God. When can I go and see the face of God?"(Ps 42:3). Here again we see the thirst within the Psalmist to be present to the Presence of God.

Describing the wonder of the Incarnation, St. John proclaims, "We saw his glory…." (Jn 1:14). The longing to see God was fulfilled at the Incarnation. Jesus, knowing this longing of people to see God face to face, declared, "Whoever has seen me has seen the Father" (Jn 14:9). And in His marvelous plan of instituting the Eucharist, Jesus made it possible for all the people, all through the centuries to have the Presence of God. St. John has recorded for us the Discourse on the Bread of Life. This discourse affirms that the Eucharist is what is going to save us from dying. Jesus says about this Bread, "One may eat it and not die" (Jn 6:50b). And the discourse has again the emphatic assurance, "Whoever eats my flesh and drinks my blood has eternal life, and I will raise him on the last day" (Jn 6:54). So, in the Eucharist, we not only have the "face to face" experience of God's presence but also the assurance of our rising with Jesus, and the Resurrection of Jesus attested this assurance once for all.

St. Paul's words attest to the fact of newness of life: "We were indeed buried with him through baptism into death so that as Christ was raised from the dead by the glory of the Father, we too might live in newness of life" (Rom 6:4). Here we understand

St. Paul's strong conviction about the effect of our own baptism. By our baptism we inherited the mystical union with Christ. His life, crucifixion, death and Resurrection are not merely past events; rather they have the unique but mystical union with us. That is why St. Paul declares, "I have been crucified with Christ; yet I live, no longer I but Christ lives in me..." (Gal 2:19b-20a). This declaration of mystical union was something that was unheard of, and thanks to St. Paul we have such a profound reality. As Albert Schweitzer put it, *"Pauline mysticism runs thus: I am in Christ; in Him I know myself as a being who is raised above this sensuous, sinful and transient world and already belong to the transcendent; in Him I am assured of resurrection; in Him I am the Child of God."*[2] The mystical effect of the Resurrection is such now each of us has "died and risen" to a new life through our own Baptism.

St. Paul further affirms the purpose of new life, "Whether we live or die we are the Lord's" (Rom 14:8). The new life of living and dying for Christ is empowered by His Presence of the Eucharist. In other words, we who belong to His Presence have the assurance not only to live with Him but also to die with Him and rise with Him. Here on earth we already belong to God in Christ. The Eucharistic Presence mystically connects each of us to Christ's sufferings. Whether it is sickness or aging, death has no longer power over us. It is in the Eucharistic Presence God is for us. And so St. Paul himself encourages us to face the reality of death boldly as, " It is Christ who dies, rather was raised, who also is at the right hand of God, who indeed intercedes for us. What will separate us from the love of Christ? Will anguish, or distress or persecution, or famine or nakedness or peril or the sword?" (Rom7:34, 35).

Thus, we who live in Christ's Eucharistic Presence have the "face to face" experience of God here on earth will have the everlasting "face to face" experience. As it is revealed to us in the Book of Revelation, the Eucharistic Presence continues in the everlasting life. The Book of Revelation describes the Eucharistic Presence as the "Throne of God" and the "Lamb" (Rev 22:1). The *throne of God* is the Presence of God and the *Lamb* is Christ. "They will look upon his face, and his name will be on their foreheads" (Rev22:4). While we see Jesus face to face in a mystical manner in the Eucharist, we will see Him face to face as He is (1Jn 3:2b).

My Personal Context:

The conviction of dying to rise with Him is what is behind challenging the reality of death. And the Eucharistic Presence is an assurance for me to live in His Presence and to die in His Presence. Let the daring examples of the Apostles dying for Christ be my inspiration. Let St. Stephen's (Acts7:55) words- *Lord Jesus receive my spirit*- be written in my mystical wish. Let

Archbishop Oscar Romero's conviction-*I do not believe in death without resurrection-*[3]be my guiding force. Let the prayer of the Church-*Lord God Your son Jesus Christ gave us the sacrament of his body and blood to guide us on our pilgrim way to your kingdom-*[4] lead me to the Eucharistic celebration.

Meditation:

After the preparatory steps:

I am conscious of mystical union with Christ. I am now face to face with Jesus. Jesus' Presence within me gives me the pledge of His Presence here. Let me be faithful to His presence till I see Him as He is. For this grace, let me now pray: *Lord Jesus Christ, let Your Presence within me guide me to be faithful to you. Let my dying glorify Your Presence as I await the glory of the risen life, where I will see you face to face. Let me join the Psalmist to sing:*

> *For my soul has been freed from death,*
> *My eyes from tears, my feet from stumbling.*
> *I shall walk before the LORD*
> *In the land of the living (Ps 116:8,9).*

51. I Shall Be His Witness

God will be seen in ordinary experience when
ordinary experience is fully open to Him.

Ronald Rolheiser[1]

*John and Nancy are daily communicants. They invite me
to go out for dinner. They have a remarkable gesture at the
dinner table to say grace before we begin to eat. One time my
bishop visited me from India. They were generous to invite the
bishop and me. It was a busy restaurant with so many tables.
They asked the Bishop to say grace. When the bishop said the
grace, John and Nancy as usual bowed the heads in reverence to
join the grace. I could notice the witness value of this gesture to
others, whose body language approved in respect for saying
grace.*

*Gino is a sacristan for more than 25 years. He opens the
Church every Sunday for the first mass at 7:30. After opening the
church he sets up for the mass, and then he sits and recites the
holy rosary. When the priest shows up in the sacristy for mass,
he would get up out of respect to wish Good morning. One time I
said to him, "Gino, I know you find it difficult to get up as you
have the bad knee. You don't have to get up to greet me." He
said, "No.. no.. This is the way I was taught to show respect."
He added smilingly, "You know, Father, I wanted to be a priest.*

It did not happen. That is another reason why I get up to greet you priests."

Gino's way of "getting up" from the chair to show respect to a priest is a Christian witness. The way of "bowing the heads" by John and Nancy for grace is a witness. Witnessing is not about great accomplishments. Witnessing is about ordinary ways of experiencing God's Presence in us.

The word *witness* has a legal connotation in our culture. In the OT, this word implies a profound sense of God's Presence as testimony to something or somebody. The Book of Genesis has the interesting story of Laban and Jacob in Chapter 31. Laban asked Jacob, "Come, then we will make a pact, you and I; the LORD shall be a witness between us" (Gen 31:44). It is a remarkable way of showing their trust in the Lord's Presence. In God's witnessing presence, Laban and Jacob made memorial stones and mounds, and they agreed, "This mound shall be witness from now on between you and me" (v 48). Again Laban said to Jacob, "...God will be witness between you and me" (v.50). This story gives us a clear indication of how they trust in God's Presence as their witness.

Inasmuch as the OT people had trust in God's Presence as a witness, God asked the people themselves to be a witness. "You are my witness, says the LORD, my servants whom I have chosen to know and believe in me and understand that it is I" (Is

43:10). "You are my witnesses, says the Lord. I am God, yes, from eternity I am He" (Is 43:12b, 13). Here we see a transition from God as witness to people as witness. In other words, God is asking people to be a witness to His witness.

This transition echoes in Jesus' words to His disciples. After the Resurrection, Jesus was with the disciples for forty days. And before ascending to His Father, Jesus said to His disciples, "You are witnesses of these things. And I am sending the promise of my Father upon you; but stay in the city until your are clothed with power on high"(Lk 24:48). St. Luke also reports this in the Acts of the Apostles, "You will receive power when the holy Spirit comes upon you, and you will be witnesses in Jerusalem, throughout Judea and Samaria and to the ends of the earth" (Acts 1:8).The Holy Spirit is the Presence of His risen Power, and for which and with which we will be witnesses.

How do we become His witness? We become His witnesses by His Presence within us. We have been given His Holy Spirit. Jesus Himself referred to this day of sending His Spirit to us. "On that day you will realize that I am in the Father and you are in me and I in you" (Jn 14:20). His risen power, the Holy Spirit is within us. St John affirms, "Now the testimony of God is this, that he has testified on behalf his Son. Whoever believes in the Son of God has this testimony within himself"

(1Jn 5:8b). Thereby we witness to His Presence with His own Presence.

What works have we to do as His witness? Christ within us is the one who said, "The works I do in my Father's name testify to me" (Jn 10:25). Jesus was always aware of the fact that His Father was always working in and through Him. Jesus said, "The works that the Father gave me to accomplish, these works that I perform testify on my behalf that the Father has sent me" (Jn 5:36). The Father accomplished all His works in and through His Son. Jesus sent His Spirit to indwell in us so that we too might accomplish His works. The works are the love of God and love of neighbor. As St John says, "If you love one another, God remains in us and his love is brought to perfection" (1Jn 4:12b). Anything done for God and for others is the work of witness.

The works of witness may involve great risk and danger to life. It is interesting to note that the Greek word for witness is *martys*, which is transliterated in English as martyr. Martyr is the one who is willing even to die for faith. Witness is the unyielding mind and heart to the external threats of life by remaining loyal to God. In extraordinary circumstances this type of witness is called for from those who follow Christ. In ordinary circumstances the witness is to do what simple things we can do for God and for others.

These works need not be great accomplishments. Every little thing we can do for God and for others is the witness. When we receive the Eucharist we become His witnesses because of God's Presence in us. The Holy Spirit empowers us to live for Him and to die for Him. That is why St. Paul said, "So whether you eat or drink, or whatever you do, do everything for the Glory of God" (1Cor 10:31). Every ordinary experience is a Eucharistic experience.

Like the OT people who sought God's Presence for witness, we seek Eucharist for witness. Like that of the OT, where God asked people to be His witness, Eucharistic Presence makes us His witness. When we receive Eucharist, as many spiritual authors say, we become what we eat. St. Leo the Great said, "For the effect of our sharing in the body and blood of Christ is to change us into what we receive. As we have died with him, and have been buried with him, so we bear him within us, both in body and spirit, in everything we do."[2] And so we become God's Presence to others. What we do to others mystically connects others to the Eucharist, and so to God. Thus everything we do is a witness with His Presence, in His Presence and for His Presence.

My Personal Context:

At the celebration of the Eucharist, I join others "Amen" to the most profound proclamation, which is known as doxology.

That is "Through Him, with him, in Him, in the unity of the Holy Spirit, all glory and honor is yours, almighty Father, for ever and ever." My "Amen" is the most holy affirmation of my witness to God. It is because I affirm the work being accomplished by the Trinity in the world, of which I am an ordinary witness.

Meditation:

After the preparatory steps:

I have now become God's witness. Christ is within me. His Presence within me makes me all the more His witness. Let me be aware of my life that should transform my work, my actions, my relation for the greater glory of God. Let me pray: *Lord Jesus, make me conscious of Your Presence in me always. Let all within me cry out "Amen" to Your Presence; let my life be a witness to Your Presence. Let me join the Psalmist to sing and walk in the ways of God:*

> *Happy are all who fear the Lord*
> *Who walk in the ways of God (128:1).*

52. *I AM in Me*

The completely human heart of the God-man
so wants the greatest possible union with us
that he calls upon the fullness of his divine
Power to make the incredible real.

Basil Pennington[1]

The kindergarten teacher, Sharon at St Mary's School, asked me to be one of the readers for her class at the school. I was given the book: **I Wanted to Know All About God**-*by Virginia L. Kroll & Dera Reid Jenkins. It is one of Eerdmans Books for young Readers. As I was reading this book to these little children, I asked them, "Where is God?" Little Leanna with all her innocence raised her hand and said, "God is in my heart." Pleasantly surprised at her response, I asked, Leanna, "How do you know God is in your heart?" She replied, "I can feel God." She said this by touching the left side of her chest and went on to say, "I can feel God with my heart beat."*

The following Sunday I saw Leanna coming out of the church after the Mass. I asked her parents, "You know Leanna was amazing in her reply. How did she get this idea that the beating of the heart is the feeling of God within us?" Leanna's mother, Alicia expressed her surprise: "I and my husband Andrew always teach our kids that God is with us. I don't know how she got this knowledge to feel God within her heart beat."

335

Leanna's gesture and understanding is typical of Christian tradition that holds the Heart as the dwelling place of God. In experiencing God within, man reveres his heart as the inner most domain of God's Presence.

When Moses asked God for his name, God replied, "I am who am" (Ex 3:14). Why was Moses curious to know the name of God? It is because he belonged to a time and culture surrounded by many pagan cultures. Pagans like Canaanites, Egyptians, Phoenicians, Greeks, Romans, etc. had many gods and goddesses. Each of them was given a mythical name. Names were necessary, as they had to be identified with their work boundaries like land, sea, and underworld. Also, the names were necessary as they had their own counterparts in the other culture. Each had sectarian tasks; interference with other gods' tasks ended in fights and death among them. Depending on the place and boundary, a god had control over other gods. At the invocation of their names, the kings were supposed to possess them and to be possessed by them.

In contrast to these pagan gods and goddesses, our God is One and He alone is God as revealed to Moses. When asked for the name, God reveals it as I AM, because God does not need a name to be identified like pagan gods. "I AM" reveals the essence of God, rather than the identity of His name. Unlike the pagan gods, who are confined to only their boundaries, God is omnipresent. Unlike the pagan gods who have power only to do their own task, God is Omnipotent. Unlike the pagan gods, who were created by kings, God is Self-existent. Unlike the pagan gods, who fight and die, God is Eternal. So "I AM" has the essence of these and other characteristics of God. Yet, in the course of the OT history, people called upon God by names, which mainly ascribe *the characteristics of God*. For example, *El Elyon* means God is Most High (Gen 14:18); *Elohim* means God Creator, Mighty and Powerful (Gen 2:4); *Adoni* means God is Lord (Gen 15:2); *El Shaddi* means God Almighty (Gen 17:1); *Jehovah-Rophe* means God heals (Ex 15:22). Even the "name" YHWH, many Scholars believe is meant to praise God's self-existence; that is, God's existence does not depend on anyone.

With the understanding of what these names mean, St. John sums up all the characteristics of "I AM" to proclaim that God is Logos. Again, it is not God's name. Logos literally means, "speaking." Logos was with God as God "spoke" to create the world. Logos is the creative word in the world. In the incarnation of Logos, God Himself gives the name: Jesus (Lk 1:31). As Pope Benedict XVI says, "In Him the meaning of the discussion of the name of God has reached its goal, and so too has that which was always meant and intended by the idea of the name of God. God has really become He who can be invoked. In Him, God has entered forever into existence with us. The name is no longer just a word at which we clutch; it is now flesh of our flesh, bone of our bone. God is for us."[2] In other words, in Jesus, "I AM" dwells within us.

Jesus, during his life and mission, that is, before his death and resurrection, testified to His essence of I AM. Jesus referring to the worship of Spirit and truth to the Samaritan woman says, "I am He..." (Jn 4:26). By this, Jesus reveals Him as **one true God to be worshipped in Spirit and truth**. Jesus walking on the sea, says, "Take courage, It is I, do not be afraid" (Mk 6:50). By this, Jesus reveals Himself as **God who transcends place and space to save others**. Referring to His death on the cross, He says, "When you lift up the son of man, then you will realize that I AM" (Jn 8:28). Here Jesus reveals **His saving power of His death and resurrection**. Talking to the Jews about Father Abraham, Jesus says, "Amen, amen, I say to you, before Abraham came to be, I AM (Jn 8:58). Here Jesus refers to **His Pre-existence**. And there are many other "I AM" statements of Jesus, such as "I am the Light of the world" (Jn 8:12), "I am the way, and the truth and life" (Jn 14:6). All these manifest the power of Jesus as I AM. These "I AM" statements, above all, proved **His oneness with His Father-"Father and I are one"** (Jn 10:30).

At the Last Supper discourses, Jesus manifests His oneness with His Father. Jesus prays to His Father, "that they all be one, as you, Father are in me and I in you, that they may be in us" (Jn 17:21). This is to effect in us the same mystical oneness Jesus has with His Father. After the resurrection, Jesus affirms it again saying, "Peace be with you. As the Father has sent me, so I send you" (Jn 20.21). It is the powerful manifestation of bestowing upon His disciples the mystical oneness He has with His Father. And his command to His disciples to preach "...in his name to all the nations..." (Lk 24:47) spells out the presence of "I Am" that would be present with them.

Jesus is the Christ; and so He is now I AM in the church. He is mystically one with the Church; He is mystically one within every member of the church. When one of them is glorified, Christ is glorified. When one of them is persecuted, Christ is persecuted. That is why Jesus said to Saul, "I am Jesus whom you are persecuting" (Acts 9:5). That is why Saul becoming St. Paul would declare "He is the head of the Body, the Church" (Eph 1:18, cf. Eph 1:23). Jesus Christ, the I AM, is mystically binding all of us into His own Body, the mystical Body of Christ.

The Church as the Mystical Body is nourished by His own Presence in the Eucharist. Jesus himself assured of His life that comes from the Eucharistic Presence: "Amen, amen, I say to you, unless you eat the flesh of the Son of Man and drink his blood, you do not have life within you" (Jn 6:53). That is why we experience Eucharistic Presence as the source and life of our life (Vat II, LG # 11, Catechism of the C C.#1324). As Pope John Paul II said, "The Church draws her life from the Eucharist."[3] God, who is the source and life, is joyfully being experienced in the Eucharist, as the source and summit.

My Personal Context:

God, the I AM, is the source and life. In giving me the Eucharist, Jesus said, "I AM the Bread of life. When I receive the Eucharist, "I AM" is within me. "Within" is the inner domain. I shall identify my heart as the inner domain for I AM to dwell within me. When I receive the Eucharist, as St. Gaudentius says, "We hold it in our hands, we receive it in our mouths, and we accept it in our hearts."[4]

Meditation:

After the preparatory steps:

As I was created to share the divinity of God, so I have the fulfillment of having Christ within me. Christ is the I AM, who is within me. Let me pray: *Lord Jesus Christ, I thank you for your abiding Presence within me. Let my life always profess the eternal Presence and the life you have destined for me. I shall join the Psalmist:*

> *For in God our hearts rejoice;*
> *In your holy name we trust (33:21)*

Notes:
Chapter 48
1. Kathy Coffy, *The Art of Faith* (, New London, CT:23rd Publication, 2007), p.105.
2. Enrico mazza, *the celebration of the Eucharist*, (Minnesota: The liturgical press, 1999), p.286
Chapter 49
1. Abbot Marmion's Quote taken from Archbishop Dolan's *Priests for the Third millennium* (Hunigton, IN: Our Sunday Visitor, 2000), p.204
2. Pope John Paul II, encyclical on Ecclesia de Eucharistia, 2003 #18
3. St Ephraim's' quote taken from Priests *for the third millennium,* p. 204
Chapter 50
1. Scott Hann, *The Lamb's Supper*, (NY: Doubleday, 1999, p.163
2. Albert Acheitzer, at www.home-pcicys.net.
3. Oscar Romero'quote: at www. Missionlocal.org
4. Ref: Funeral mass-post com.prayer.
Chapter 51
1. Ronald Rolheiser, *the Shattered lantern*, (The crossword publishing co., 2004) p.63
2. St. Leo, the Great. *The liturgy of Hours*, Vol.II, (NY:Catholic book publishing,1976),p.660.
Chapter 52
1. Basil Pennington, *Journey in a holy land*, (Brewster, MS: Paraclete Press, 2006), p.143.
2. Ratzinger, *Introduction to Christianity*, (NY: Herder and Herder, 1970), p.92
3. Pope John Paul II, *Ecclesia de Eucharistia*, 2003, #1
4. St. Gaudentius, *The liturgy of Hours, Vol.II*, (NY: Catholic book publishing, 1976), p.670.